True Tales from the Seas

Henry Billings

Melissa Stone Billings

STECK-VAUGHN
COMPANY

A Division of Harcourt Brace & Company

www.steck-vaughn.com

Acknowledgments

Executive Editor: Stephanie Muller
Senior Editor: Kristy Schulz
Project Editor: Meredith Edgley O'Reilly
Associate Director of Design: Cynthia Ellis
Design Manager: Alexandra Corona
Media Researcher: Claudette Landry
Electronic Production Artists: Dina Instinski, Linda Reed
Electronic Production Specialist: Alan Klemp

Cartography: MapQuest.com, Inc.
Illustration Credits: Pp. 89, 108(b), 109(m,b) Kathie Kelleher
Photo Credits: Cover (inset) ©The Palm Beach Post; Cover (compass) CORBIS/Dorling Kindersley Limited, London; Cover (background), p.1 CORBIS/Paul A. Souders; Cover (life preserver, passport), p.3 ©PhotoDisc; p.6 ©John Lancaster/H.M. Bark Endeavour Foundation; p.8 Culver Pictures; p.9(l) CORBIS/Brandon D. Cole; p.9(r) CORBIS/Yann Arthus-Bertrand; p.10 CORBIS/Michael Freeman; p.14 Courtesy The Atlantic Mutual Companies; p.16 North Wind Picture Archives; p.17 CORBIS/Wolfgang Kaehler; p.18 Peabody Essex Museum, Salem, MA. Photo by Mark Secton; pp.22, 24 Old Dartmouth Historical Society/New Bedford Whaling Museum; p.25 Jackson Collection, Courtesy Peabody Essex Museum, Salem, MA; p.30 Christie's Images; p.32 Brown Brothers; p.33 Archive Photos (Popperfoto); p.34(l) CORBIS/Bettmann; p.34(r) The Everett Collection; pp.38, 40, 41 Naval Historical Foundation; p.46 The Kon-Tiki Museum, Oslo, Norway; p.48 CORBIS/Buddy Mays; p.49 The Kon-Tiki Museum, Oslo, Norway; p.50(t) ArchivePhotos/Camera Press; p.50(b) The Kon-Tiki Museum, Oslo, Norway; p.54 ©Phil Bray/The Everett Collection; p.56 UPI/Corbis-Bettmann; p.57 ©Phil Bray/The Everett Collection; p.58(both) UPI/Corbis-Bettmann; p.62 ©James Watt/Animals Animals; pp.64, 65, 66 CORBIS/Jeffrey L. Rotman; p.70 ©The Palm Beach Post; p.72 ©Lynn Pelham/Sports Illustrated; p.73 ©Herb Segars/Animals Animals; p.74 ©John Lopinot/The Palm Beach Post; pp.78, 80, 81 Sovfoto/Eastfoto; p.82 ©Zig Leszczynski/Animals Animals; p.86 CORBIS/Joel W. Rogers; p.88 CORBIS/Jack Fields; p.90 AP/Wide World; p.94 CORBIS/Catherine Karnow; p.96 ©The Palm Beach Post; p.97 AP/Wide World; p.98 ©Allsport; p.108(t) ©PhotoDisc; p.108(m) CORBIS/Nik Wheeler; p.109(t) ©Photo Researchers.

Contents

NORTH
AMERICA

SOUTH
AMERICA

PACIFIC

OCEAN

ATLANTIC

OCEAN

ATLANTIC

OCEAN

Bering
Strait

Beaufort
Sea

Baffin
Bay

Bering
Sea

Hudson
Bay

Gulf of
Alaska

Gulf of
Mexico

Straits of
Florida

Caribbean Sea

Equator

Strait of
Magellan

Cape Horn

of the World

ARCTIC
OCEAN

wegian
Sea

EUROPE

Black Sea

Mediterranean Sea

AFRICA

Red Sea

ea

Cape of
Good Hope

ASIA

Sea
of
Okhotsk

Sea
of
Japan

Yellow
Sea

East
China
Sea

South
China
Sea

Arabian
Sea

Bay
of
Bengal

Andaman
Sea

PACIFIC

OCEAN

INDIAN

OCEAN

Timor
Sea

AUSTRALIA

Great Barrier Reef

Coral
Sea

Tasman
Sea

N
W   E
S

ANTARCTICA

Into the Unknown

Captain James Cook opened the sealed envelope. The top secret orders told the English captain to sail his ship *Endeavour* to the South Pacific Ocean. There, Cook was to look for the mysterious "southern **continent**." Some people said this body of land was even larger than Europe and Asia put together. Though the *Endeavour* **crew** would never find such a place, their journey would take them into dangerous, unknown waters.

To Australia

Cook's search for the southern continent began in 1768. During the journey he explored and **charted**, or mapped, the two main islands of New Zealand. Then in April 1770, he began to sail along the eastern coast of Australia.

By May, Cook had charted much of the eastern coast. The coast was on the *Endeavour*'s left. On the right, Cook soon saw a long **reef**, which today is called the Great Barrier Reef. It is an amazing 1,250 miles long.

The Great Barrier Reef is a sailor's nightmare. It is made of very sharp coral. The **coral** could easily rip the bottom out of a ship. As the Great Barrier Reef stretches north, it bends closer and closer to the coast of Australia. Any ship caught sailing north between the coast and the reef has less and less room to move. If Captain Cook had known what he was getting into, he might have turned the *Endeavour* around right away.

Cook charted the Australian coast, not knowing the dangers that lay ahead.

Sailing into Trouble

Soon Cook saw trouble everywhere. To the north and east, he spotted tiny islands of coral. Cook could steer the ship to avoid what he could see. But there were ten times as many coral reefs that he couldn't see. Many were covered by only a few feet of water. Hitting any could sink his ship and drown his crew.

Very worried, Cook sent a small boat out ahead of the *Endeavour*. Its crew tested the water's **depth** and signaled the information to Cook. But the bottom of the ocean kept changing. One minute it was deep enough. The next minute it was very shallow. Cook never knew for sure which way he should steer.

Cook kept looking for a way out to the open sea. He knew there was a **strait**, or narrow body of water, between Australia and New Guinea. Today, it is called the Torres Strait. What Cook didn't know, however, was that it was still hundreds of miles to the north.

At last, the men on the small boat reported that the sea was more than a hundred feet deep. Minutes passed, and the depth didn't change. Night came. Hoping the danger was over, Cook told part of his crew to go to bed. Less than two hours later, there was a loud thud. The worst had happened. The *Endeavour* had hit the reef. The ship was now stuck. It was jammed into the coral and leaking badly.

Getting Free

Huge waves battered the poor ship back and forth. Cook could hear the reef grinding away at his ship's bottom. He knew that the ship would soon break apart and sink. The crew used ropes to try to pull the ship off the reef. That didn't work.

Then Cook ordered his men to toss guns, oil jars, and many other things over the ship's side. If they could lighten the ship, maybe it would float off the reef with the next high **tide**. That didn't work, either. Meanwhile, the rising water rushed into the ship. The men worked hard to get the water out.

All day Cook remained calm. Somehow he kept his crew calm, too. He reminded them that the next high tide would come late that night. It would be a few feet higher than the one during the day. Maybe that high tide would free the ship.

The Great Barrier Reef is beautiful to see, but the coral can destroy ships.

Cook's top secret orders had put the *Endeavour* in terrible danger.

The extra few feet of water did make the difference. The water lifted the ship off the reef. But Cook now faced a new problem. The steady rocking against the reef had made the hole in the ship's bottom much larger. The *Endeavour* was still 25 miles from land, and water was quickly entering the ship.

The men worked the **pumps** as hard as they could. They moved water out as fast as it rushed in. But the men quickly became tired.

Then one of Cook's crew had a great idea. He and the other men used ropes to lower a big piece of a sail beneath the ship. Once the sail covered the hole, the force that pulled in the water also pulled in the sail. It worked. The sail plugged the hole. The ship still leaked a bit. Now, though, it took only one pump instead of three to keep the ship floating on the water. The *Endeavour* headed to shore.

Later, Captain James Cook had the hole properly fixed. He then continued his **voyage** of discovery, finishing in 1771. Even though Cook never found the "southern continent," Cook learned much about the South Pacific and Australia. The voyage was a success.

Read and Remember — Finish the Sentence

Circle the best ending for each sentence.

1. James Cook explored the waters around _____.
   Africa   Australia   North America

2. Cook tried to stay in deep water to avoid the _____.
   Great Barrier Reef   sharks   tide

3. The *Endeavour* was in danger of _____.
   burning   sinking   being attacked

4. Cook hoped that his ship would be freed by the _____.
   strait   rising water   shallow water

5. Cook's men plugged a hole in the ship with a piece of _____.
   sail   rubber   net

Write About It

Imagine you were one of the men sailing with James Cook. Write a letter home, describing what you did when the *Endeavour* became stuck on the coral reef.

Dear _____,

_____

_____

_____

_____

_____

_____

USE WHAT YOU KNOW

Focus on Vocabulary — Make a Word

Choose a word in dark print to complete each sentence. Write the letters of the word on the blanks. When you are finished, the letters in the circles will tell you which ocean Cook explored.

pumps	**charted**	**crew**	**coral**
strait	**voyage**	**depth**	**tide**
reef	**continent**		

1. Cook was looking for a new _____, or large body of land.

2. Cook _____, or mapped, two islands of New Zealand.

3. The men tested the _____ of the water.

4. The men used _____ to get water out of the ship.

5. Cook's sea _____ took three years.

6. _____ is the skeletons of tiny sea animals.

7. Cook's ship was far from the _____ near New Guinea.

8. The *Endeavour* got caught on a dangerous _____.

9. Cook and his men waited for a high _____.

10. Cook tried to keep members of his _____ calm.

Continents and Oceans

Captain James Cook explored the Pacific Ocean, one of Earth's large bodies of water. Earth also has large bodies of land called **continents**. Look at the map of the world below. Write the answer to each question.

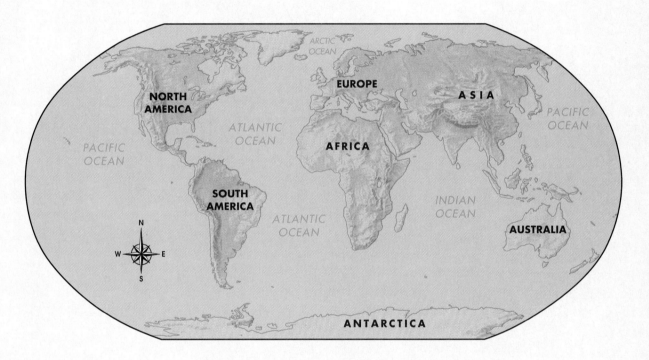

1. What are the names of the four oceans? _____

_____

2. What are the names of the seven continents? _____

_____

3. Which five continents are along the Pacific Ocean? _____

_____

4. Which two oceans are along Africa? _____

5. Which ocean is along Asia, North America, and Europe? _____

6. Which ocean separates South America and Africa? _____

Captain Mary

Neptune's Car was a beautiful sight to see as it left New York City on July 1, 1856. All the sails of the great **clipper ship** were up and catching the wind. Neptune's Car was headed for San Francisco, California. To get there, the ship would have to sail all the way around South America. It would travel in both the Atlantic and Pacific oceans. It would be no pleasure trip. The ship would be sailing through some of the roughest waters in the world.

A Woman at Sea

The captain of Neptune's Car was Joshua Patten. He had taken command of the ship in 1853, at age 26. Joshua hadn't wanted to leave his wife behind. So he asked the ship's owners if Mary could come with him. They agreed.

Joshua sailed Neptune's Car all over the world. While traveling he taught Mary how to **navigate,** or guide, the ship. He showed her how to write all the details of the voyage in the **logbook**. Mary never thought she would use what she learned, though. In those days, women simply did not sail ships. But Mary enjoyed life at sea and was eager to learn the skills needed to navigate the ship.

When Neptune's Car headed for San Francisco three years later, it carried a **cargo** worth about $350,000. That's well over $10 million in today's dollars. So Joshua wanted to reach San Francisco quickly and safely. Fortunately, Joshua's clipper ship was one of the fastest ships around.

The seas near the tip of South America were very rough.

Trouble on Board

After *Neptune's Car* left New York City, strong winds drove it south toward the **equator**. The ship was making good time. But then a problem developed on board. Joshua found out that the **First Mate** sometimes slept when he was supposed to be working. Joshua also had other problems with the First Mate. When Joshua went to sleep, the First Mate lowered some of the sails, slowing the ship down. The two men argued many times. Finally, Joshua fired the First Mate and placed him under **arrest**.

Joshua didn't choose anyone else to be First Mate. He didn't think anyone else could do the job. So Joshua began doing both the job of the captain and the job of the First Mate.

As September came, the ship neared the rough seas off the tip of South America. The ship had to sail around the **cape**, a bit of land that stuck out into the sea. This was the dangerous Cape Horn. The icy and windy continent of Antarctica was not far away. Huge waves crashed around the ship and Cape Horn as the sea rushed up from Antarctica. Strong winds rocked the ship. It seemed that only a captain as good as Joshua could keep the ship on course.

It was difficult to work two jobs, and it finally got to Captain Patten. He fell ill and was too sick to do his job. By then, Mary was expecting a baby. Still, she boldly stepped forward to take command of the ship.

On to San Francisco

When the First Mate heard that Mary was taking command, he offered to take over. Mary refused. The First Mate then began to try to take control of the ship. It seemed that there might be a **mutiny**. The whole crew might decide to rise up against Mary. Bravely, Mary gathered the men together right away and asked for their help. The crew agreed. One reporter later wrote that the men agreed "to stand by her and the ship, come what might."

Mary Patten realized that it might be wise to head for the nearest **port**. But Mary knew that Joshua wouldn't want this. He would want the cargo taken to San Francisco. She decided that she would keep *Neptune's Car* going along its planned route.

Mary Patten's ability to navigate came in very handy. To get around Cape Horn, she needed all the skills that Joshua had taught her. For 18 days the sea

Mary Patten navigated *Neptune's Car* around Cape Horn.

pounded the ship. Huge waves broke over the deck. Winds ripped at the sails. It was one of Cape Horn's worst seasons ever. How Mary got *Neptune's Car* around the cape was better than anything found in a storybook, wrote one man later.

"Captain Mary" was busy every minute. She had to navigate the ship. She had to write details in the logbook. She also had to take care of Joshua. At times, he seemed better. Then he would get very ill again. Soon he became both deaf and blind. For 50 straight days and nights, Mary didn't even have time to change her clothes.

Mary's hard work kept the crew going. Each man did his part to make sure the ship got to San Francisco safely. Whatever Mary asked the crew to do, they were very willing to work hard to get it done.

At last, *Neptune's Car* neared California. To honor Mary, the crew cleaned and shined the ship. They reached their port on November 15, 1856. The voyage had taken 136 days. Joshua was still very ill, and Mary was worn out. But she had done it. Captain Mary had guided *Neptune's Car* safely to San Francisco.

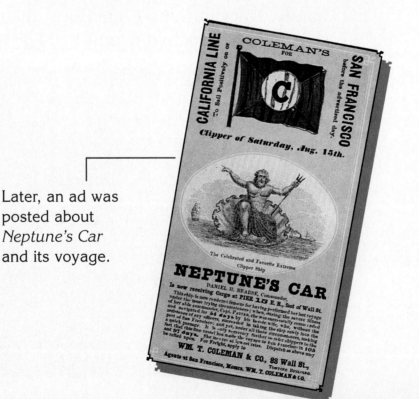

Later, an ad was posted about *Neptune's Car* and its voyage.

USE WHAT YOU KNOW

Read and Remember — Choose the Answer

Draw a circle around the correct answer.

1. Around which continent did *Neptune's Car* sail?

   Africa   Australia   South America

2. Who taught Mary Patten to navigate?

   Joshua Patten   the First Mate   her father

3. Whom did Joshua Patten fire during the voyage?

   the captain   the cook   the First Mate

4. Which words best describe the waters around Cape Horn?

   calm and clear   cold and rough   warm and shallow

5. What did Mary ask the crew to do?

   choose a new captain   help her   leave the ship

6. Which place did *Neptune's Car* finally reach?

   Africa   California   New York City

Think About It — Fact or Opinion

A **fact** is a true statement. An **opinion** is a statement that tells what a person thinks. Write **F** beside each statement that is a fact. Write **O** beside each statement that is an opinion.

_____ 1. *Neptune's Car* was headed for San Francisco.

_____ 2. Women make better ship captains than men do.

_____ 3. Joshua should have brought a good doctor on the trip.

_____ 4. Joshua became both deaf and blind.

_____ 5. Mary Patten kept the ship going along the route as planned.

_____ 6. The men on *Neptune's Car* deserved medals.

USE WHAT YOU KNOW

Focus on Vocabulary — Finish the Paragraphs

Use the words in dark print to complete the paragraphs. Reread the paragraphs to be sure they make sense.

logbook   **equator**   **navigate**   **arrest**

cape   **clipper ship**   **First Mate**   **mutiny**

port   **cargo**

Neptune's Car was a very fast (1)_____. It carried a large (2)_____ worth over $10 million in today's dollars. Captain Joshua Patten planned to sail the ship to San Francisco. To get there, the ship had to cross the (3)_____. It also had to go around a dangerous (4)_____ sticking out into the sea.

During the journey, Joshua argued with the (5)_____. Finally, Joshua had the man placed under (6)_____. Later, Joshua became ill, and Mary took control of the ship. She decided not to head for the nearest (7)_____. Instead, she wanted to finish the journey as planned. Mary feared that there might be a (8)_____ among the crew. But the men agreed to stand by her and help her. She was able to (9)_____ the ship through rough waters. She wrote down details of the trip in the ship's (10)_____. At last, she brought *Neptune's Car* safely to San Francisco.

Map Directions

The four main directions are **north**, **south**, **east**, and **west**. On maps they are shown on a **compass rose**. In-between directions are **northeast**, **southeast**, **southwest**, and **northwest**. This map shows part of South America, the continent that Mary Patten sailed around. Study the map. Circle the answer that best completes each sentence below.

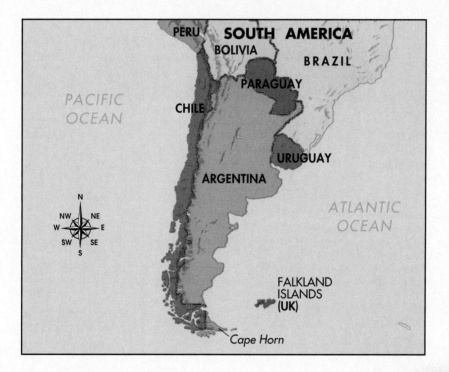

1. Cape Horn is _____ of Bolivia.

    north   south   west

2. Paraguay is east of _____.

    Chile   Uruguay   the Atlantic Ocean

3. The Falkland Islands are _____ of Cape Horn.

    southwest   northwest   northeast

4. To get from Bolivia to Uruguay, travel _____.

    southwest   northwest   southeast

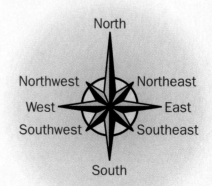

Alone at Sea

Life hadn't been too kind to American sailor Joshua Slocum. His first wife died in 1884, and his second marriage was not a happy one. Then in 1892 he sailed his ship into a **sandbar** by accident. The ship was ruined. At the age of 48, Slocum was nearly broke. Yet his life would change. In time, he would get a new boat. Then he would do something no one had ever done before. He would sail around the world all by himself.

The *Spray*

Slocum had once been the captain of a great clipper ship. But there were no jobs like that left anymore. Companies no longer wanted to send goods on ships powered by sails. They wanted ships powered by steam. Slocum thought his days at sea were over.

Then a rich friend gave Slocum a boat. It needed some repairs, the friend warned. That was putting it mildly. Slocum found the 100-year-old *Spray* rotting in a field. There wasn't much worth saving. Even so, Slocum began to fix up the old boat. It took him 13 months. He used nothing but hand tools and a steam box to bend wood. Finally, he turned the 37-foot *Spray* into a tough boat.

Slocum then made a bold move. He had already sailed around the world five times. But he had always had a crew. This time, he decided to do it alone.

Slocum knew he was **risking** his life. Still, he had hope of success. The *Spray* was small but strong. Also, Slocum knew a lot about the oceans of the world. He knew which way ocean **currents** flowed. He also knew how the winds blew in different parts of the world.

So on April 24, 1895, Slocum set sail from Boston. He crossed the Atlantic Ocean and headed for the Mediterranean Sea. When he reached Gibraltar in Europe, the people there said his small boat would be attacked by pirates. Slocum decided they were right. He sailed back across the Atlantic to South America.

Even so, one pirate ship came after him. Slocum barely got away. Luckily, a strong wind blew up. The pirate ship, which had more sails, was blown sideways. A wave hit its deck, breaking its **mast**. Slocum sailed off while the pirates struggled to save their ship.

Pirates weren't Slocum's only worry. **Boredom** was a problem, too. He spent more than 60 days at a time out on the open ocean. He had no one to talk to. Still, he found excuses to talk. Slocum talked to the moon. He gave orders to a make-believe crew. He also sang sea songs to lift his spirits.

Around South America

Slocum made three stops in South America. Then he sailed into the deadly Strait of Magellan. This 400-mile strait is a narrow strip of water between the

Joshua Slocum stands on his boat, the *Spray*.

Slocum faced pirates, outlaws, and rough winds during his voyage.

tip of South America and a group of islands. The largest island is called Tierra del Fuego, or "land of fire." Here the winds and the currents were very dangerous. The strait was feared for another reason, as well. **Outlaws** in canoes often attacked passing ships.

One day, some outlaws did approach his boat. Slocum didn't want them to know he was alone. So he made a scarecrow and dressed it up like a sailor. From a distance, it looked like a second man. Then he ran below deck, changed his clothes, and hurried up to the deck again. By doing this, he made it look like there was yet another man on board. To his relief, the outlaws turned and paddled away.

For weeks, Slocum battled the winds of the strait. At times, it seemed as if he was traveling backwards. One dark night, he became confused and turned the wrong way. He ended up in a terrible spot with waves crashing on rocks all around him. Since he couldn't see which way to go, Slocum had to steer by sound. That meant steering away from the loudest noise. "God knows how my **vessel** escaped," he later wrote.

After hours of this, Slocum sailed into a small **cove** to get some sleep. To be safe, he placed sharp tacks on the deck with the points facing up. Later that night, he woke up to the sound of screams and splashing

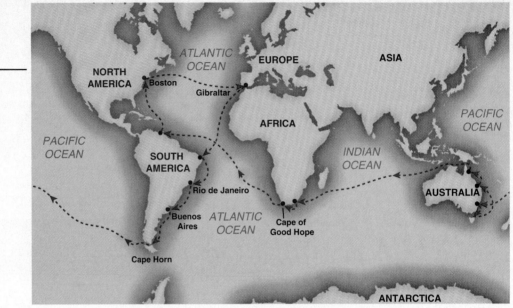

Slocum's voyage around the world took more than three years.

water. Outlaws had crept on board in bare feet. Now they were jumping over the side. After that, the outlaws didn't bother him anymore.

The Most Famous Sailor in the World

Slocum finally made it to the Pacific Ocean. He visited some Pacific islands and Australia. From there, he went on to the Indian Ocean and to Africa.

After sailing around the southern tip of Africa, Slocum headed northwest across the Atlantic. By June 27, 1898, he was home. Slocum had been at sea for 3 years, 2 months, and 3 days. He had sailed more than 46,000 miles. Slocum wrote a book about his voyage. He called it *Sailing Alone Around the World*.

Joshua Slocum became the most famous sailor of his time. For a while, he enjoyed his fame. Then he grew **restless** again. On November 14, 1909, he set sail in the *Spray* once more. By this time he was 64 years old. He told his friends he was sailing the Atlantic Ocean to South America. He wanted to find the **headwaters** of the Amazon River. No one ever saw him or his boat again. What happened to Joshua Slocum is one of the great mysteries of the sea.

USE WHAT YOU KNOW

Read and Remember — Check the Events

Place a check in front of the three sentences that tell what happened in the story.

_____ **1.** Joshua Slocum learned to sail when he was 48 years old.

_____ **2.** Slocum sailed around the world alone.

_____ **3.** It took Slocum more than three years to complete his journey.

_____ **4.** Slocum always sailed brand new boats.

_____ **5.** Outlaws and pirates tried to attack Slocum.

_____ **6.** No one wanted to hear about Slocum's voyage.

Write About It

Imagine you were a reporter in 1898. Write a short article about Joshua Slocum's journey. Tell who, what, when, where, and why in your article.

Focus on Vocabulary — Finish Up

Choose the correct word in dark print to complete each sentence.

currents	**sandbar**	**boredom**	**restless**
cove	**outlaws**	**risking**	**vessel**
mast	**headwaters**		

1. A ship or large boat is a _____.

2. People who do not follow the law are _____.

3. A tall pole that holds up a sail is called a _____.

4. When waters flow in certain directions, they form _____.

5. When you put yourself in danger, you are _____ your life.

6. Small streams that form the beginning of a river are _____.

7. A small, sheltered area of water near the shore is a _____.

8. An area of sand that builds up underwater is a _____.

9. When you are not able to relax or stay still, you feel _____.

10. _____ is what a person feels when life seems very dull.

Hemispheres

Earth can be divided into **hemispheres**. The area north of the **equator** is the Northern Hemisphere. The area south of the equator is the Southern Hemisphere. Earth can also be divided into the Eastern Hemisphere and the Western Hemisphere. Joshua Slocum sailed through all four hemispheres. Study the map of the world below. Write the answer to each question.

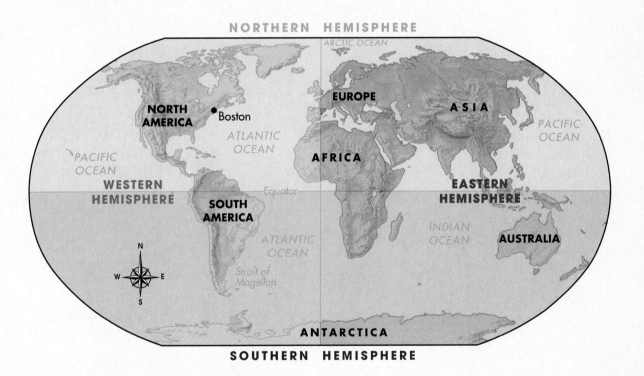

1. Is Australia in the Northern or Southern Hemisphere? _____

2. Is most of Africa in the Eastern or Western Hemisphere? _____

3. Joshua Slocum set sail from Boston. Name the two hemispheres that Boston is in. _____

4. In which three hemispheres is South America? _____

_____

The Ship That Could Not Sink

The two objects were about the same size. One was a ship called the *Titanic*, the largest ship ever built by human hands. It measured 883 feet long, about the length of three football fields. The other object was an **iceberg**, a huge block of floating ice. Most of the iceberg was underwater, so it didn't look as big as the *Titanic*. But it, too, was huge. On the night of April 14, 1912, these two objects would **collide** in the North Atlantic Ocean.

The Best of Everything

The *Titanic* was built in Belfast, Ireland. It was a fancy ship, made with the best of everything. There was heat and lighting in every cabin. The ship had a swimming pool, three restaurants, and two libraries. It also had elevators and a gym. The *Titanic* was 92 feet wide and 175 feet high. It weighed more than 46,000 tons. The ship was built so well that people called it **"unsinkable."**

The *Titanic* had room for 32 **lifeboats**. Yet it only carried 20. That was not nearly enough for all 2,228 people on board. But no one was worried. After all, most people believed nothing could sink this ship. Besides, the 20 lifeboats were more than the law required at the time.

On April 10, 1912, the *Titanic* set out on its first voyage ever. Some of the richest people in the world were aboard. Many poor **immigrants** also were aboard the *Titanic*, hoping to find better lives in America. The ship left from England. It crossed the

The *Titanic* had the best of everything, including this grand staircase.

English **Channel** to France. There it picked up more people. The *Titanic* then sailed to Ireland for another stop. After that, it headed across the Atlantic Ocean toward New York.

The first two days of travel were calm and mild. The passengers sang songs, danced, and dined. They enjoyed walking around the huge decks of the ship.

Iceberg Ahead!

By the night of April 14, the weather had turned much cooler. Most people stayed inside. The ship had entered the cold waters of the North Atlantic. Messages sent by other ships warned about icebergs in the area. But the great *Titanic* sailed into the night at full speed.

The captain of the *Titanic*, Edward Smith, warned his crew to look out for icebergs. But that was not easy to do. There was no moon, so it was very dark. Also, the sea was calm. It was as smooth as glass. Without waves splashing on the icebergs, these chunks of ice were even harder to see.

At 9:40 P.M., the *Titanic* got another iceberg warning. It was received by Jack Phillips, the man who ran the radio. Phillips just put the warning aside. He didn't have time to read it then. He was too busy sending messages for passengers. This final warning never reached Captain Smith. So no one realized just how close the icebergs were.

At 11:40 P.M., Frederick Fleet, a **lookout**, was staring at the dark and silent sea. Suddenly, he saw an iceberg. It was right in the path of the *Titanic*. Fleet quickly rang the alarm bell. The crew tried to turn the ship. But there just wasn't enough time. The ship was too big and going too fast. The *Titanic* struck the iceberg on the ship's right side. Seawater rushed into the front end of the ship. Slowly, very slowly, the "unsinkable" ship began to go down.

Death at Sea

At first, the passengers were not frightened. The members of the crew, however, knew the ship was in trouble. After looking at the damage, they told Smith that the ship wouldn't last much more than two hours. The captain called other ships for help. But no other vessels were nearby. It would be more than four hours before help finally arrived.

Meanwhile, Smith told the crew to begin loading the lifeboats. His order was clear — "Women and children first." But rich people were allowed on the boats first. Most of the poor immigrants were not allowed to come up to where the lifeboats were.

By 12:45 A.M. on April 15, the first lifeboat was lowered into the sea. The boat could carry 65 people. Yet only 28 people climbed into it. At this time, most of the people still didn't believe the *Titanic* would sink. Other ships were sure to come if there was real trouble. Besides, the band was still playing. So people waited quietly on the deck, listening to the music.

Soon, however, the ship began taking on more water. The **bow** started going down faster and faster.

One of the *Titanic*'s lifeboats

At last, the passengers began to understand what was happening. Suddenly, all the lifeboats leaving the ship were jammed with people.

At 2:05 A.M., the last lifeboat left. There were still more than 1,500 people on board the *Titanic*. Twelve minutes later, the bow sank below the surface. The **stern** was up in the air. Many people who were still on board jumped or fell into the icy, cold sea.

At 2:18 A.M., the lights on the ship went out. Two minutes later, the great *Titanic* broke in half. Finally, the stern went under. Those people still on the ship drowned. The people who had jumped or fallen into the sea slowly froze to death.

The people in lifeboats drifted in the cold sea for two hours. At last, a ship named *Carpathia* arrived. Its crew saved everyone in the lifeboats. In all, only 705 people **survived** that terrible night. Sadly, the lives of 1,523 others, including Captain Edward Smith, were lost when the "unsinkable" ship sank to the bottom of the ocean.

Captain Smith lost his life when the *Titanic* sank into the ocean.

Read and Remember — Finish the Sentence

Circle the best ending for each sentence.

1. Before April 10, 1912, the number of voyages the *Titanic* had made was _____.
   two   ten   zero

2. The *Titanic* was headed to _____.
   New York   Russia   Florida

3. The *Titanic* hit a huge iceberg _____.
   at noon   in the morning   at night

4. The first people allowed in the lifeboats were _____.
   women and children   poor people   ship officers

5. Some people got away from the sinking ship _____.
   in helicopters   in lifeboats   on rafts

6. The *Titanic* sank in the cold waters of the _____.
   Arctic Ocean   Pacific Ocean   North Atlantic Ocean

Think About It — Find the Main Ideas

Underline the two most important ideas from the story.

1. The *Titanic* had three restaurants and two libraries.

2. The *Titanic* sank after hitting an iceberg.

3. Edward Smith was the captain of the *Titanic*.

4. Many people died when the *Titanic* sank.

5. The man who ran the radio ignored the iceberg warning.

6. The *Titanic* was built in Belfast, Ireland.

USE WHAT YOU KNOW

Focus on Vocabulary — Crossword Puzzle

Use the clues to complete the puzzle. Choose from the words in dark print.

survived   **channel**   **lifeboats**   **unsinkable**

stern   **iceberg**   **collide**   **lookout**

bow   **immigrants**

Across

1. to strike or bump together

3. people who move to another country

4. not able to sink

7. person who watches for danger

8. back end of a ship

9. stayed alive

Down

1. a body of water that connects two larger bodies of water

2. small boats used for saving lives

5. very large block of floating ice

6. front end of a ship

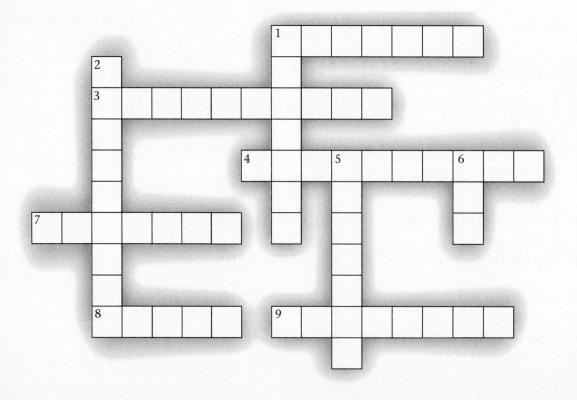

Latitude and Longitude

You can find places on globes and maps by using lines. Lines that run east to west are lines of **latitude**. Lines that run north to south are lines of **longitude**. All the lines are marked using **degrees**, or °. For example, the *Titanic* sank near the 41°N latitude and the 50°W longitude. Study the map. Circle the answer that best completes each sentence below.

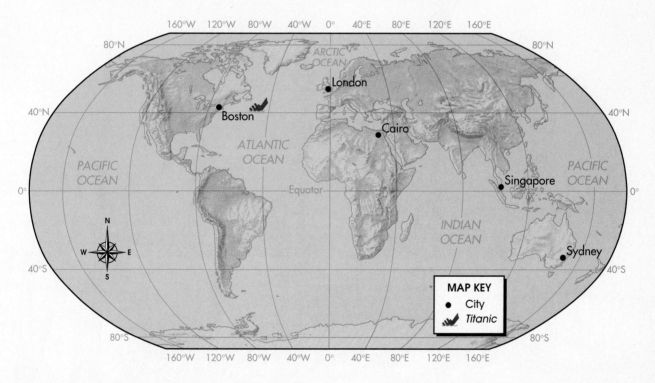

1. What is the latitude of Boston?

   42°N   120°E   25°S

2. What is the longitude of London?

   32°S   20°W   0°

3. Which city is closest to the 30°E longitude?

   Cairo   Boston   Singapore

4. Which city is closest to the equator, the 0° latitude?

   London   Singapore   Sydney

A Ship Lost

It didn't seem possible. Huge Navy ships could not just **vanish** without a trace. Yet that is what happened to the U.S.S. *Cyclops* in the middle of World War I. On March 4, 1918, the *Cyclops* left the West Indies island of Barbados and set out in the Atlantic Ocean. The ship was headed for Norfolk, Virginia. But it never arrived. One day the ship was there, and the next day it was gone.

The Ship Leaves Barbados

The U.S.S. *Cyclops* belonged to the United States Navy. For eight years this ship sailed the ocean with no problems. At 542 feet long, the ship was big enough to carry huge loads of coal and other cargo. The *Cyclops* had tall cranes bolted to its deck. These were needed to move cargo. The cranes made the *Cyclops* heavy on top. But Captain George W. Worley knew how to handle that. Worley had been in the Navy for 28 years. He had been the captain of the *Cyclops* since its very first voyage.

The weather was clear when the *Cyclops* and its crew of 309 men moved out into the Atlantic Ocean from Barbados on March 4. The ship's path took it right into the mysterious **Bermuda Triangle**. The Bermuda Triangle is an area of the Atlantic Ocean shaped by imaginary lines. The area's **boundaries** run from Florida to Bermuda to Puerto Rico.

Today, many people find the Bermuda Triangle a scary place. More than fifty ships have disappeared without a trace in this one patch of ocean. Back in 1918, though, no one had ever heard of the Bermuda Triangle. No one had any fears about sailing through these waters.

The *Cyclops*'s trip should only have taken a few days. But one of the ship's engines was not working. That slowed the vessel down. Still, the *Cyclops* should have made it to Virginia by March 13.

When it didn't arrive, the Navy started a search. It checked to see if an **S.O.S.** had been sent. Such a message would have told the Navy that the ship was in trouble. The *Cyclops* had a working radio on board. But its crew never sent an S.O.S.

The Navy also checked the ocean waters between Barbados and Virginia. Navy **officials** thought they might find the ship itself or some lifeboats filled with members of the crew. At the very least, they thought that they would find bits of the wrecked ship. They believed that no matter what had happened to the *Cyclops*, some parts of the ship or other clues would be left in the water.

The U.S.S. *Cyclops* carried coal, which was loaded on other ships at sea.

A sailor on the U.S.S. *Cyclops*

Instead, the Navy searchers found nothing in the ocean waters. Other Navy people were ordered to go to every island between Barbados and Virginia. They, too, found nothing.

Looking for Answers

No one could explain it. Some people wondered if the heavy cranes and cargo made the ship roll over and sink. Others thought that the *Cyclops* might have sunk in a storm. But the Navy stated that the weather had "not been bad and could hardly have given the *Cyclops* trouble." Later, one reporter found that there had been high winds off the coast of Virginia on March 10. But the Navy didn't think the *Cyclops* could have been that close to Virginia with one engine not working.

Some people thought the ship had hit a **mine**, a weapon that will blow up if struck. But there were no mines in those waters. Besides, the crew would have had time to send an S.O.S. Some men also would have been able to get into lifeboats.

Other people wondered about a **torpedo**. One torpedo could have blown the *Cyclops* to pieces. During World War I, Germany was an enemy of the United States. So people thought the Germans might have shot a torpedo at the ship. That didn't happen, though. No German **submarines** were in the area. After the war ended, United States officials looked at Germany's records just to be sure. The records proved that a torpedo did not hit the *Cyclops*.

Wild Stories

Then came the **theory** that the captain of the *Cyclops* had turned the ship over to the enemies of the United States. In fact, Captain Worley had been born in Germany. His real name was George Wichmann. He

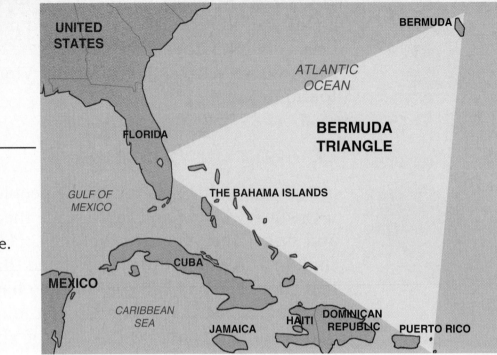

Many ships have disappeared in the mysterious Bermuda Triangle.

had changed it to "Worley" to make it sound less German. Was it possible that Worley wanted the Germans to win the war? Could he have turned and sailed the *Cyclops* into German waters?

A closer look into Worley's life showed that he was clearly a strange man. He liked to walk the deck dressed only in a hat and his long underwear. He also loved to play jokes on people. Yet he had been in the U.S. Navy for almost 30 years. There was no sign that he had been in touch with Germany. Besides, the 309 men on board with him never would have let him deliver them to the enemy.

Some of the theories about the *Cyclops* grew really wild. A few people thought there had been a mutiny by the crew. Someone said the ship might have been hit by a giant wave. One writer thought that a huge octopus might have pulled the ship to the bottom of the ocean.

In the end, no one could say for sure why the *Cyclops* had disappeared. Navy officials called it "one of the most **baffling** mysteries" ever. The lost ship became one of the Bermuda Triangle mysteries that could not be solved.

USE WHAT YOU KNOW

Read and Remember — Choose the Answer

Draw a circle around the correct answer.

1. What was not working on the U.S.S. *Cyclops*?

   a crane   one engine   the torpedoes

2. Through which area did the path of the *Cyclops* go?

   Indian Ocean   Gulf of Mexico   Bermuda Triangle

3. What was found in the water where the *Cyclops* disappeared?

   pieces of the ship   empty lifeboats   nothing

4. Which was given as a possible theory for what had happened to the Navy ship?

   German attack   fire on board   iceberg in path

5. What did Navy officials call the case?

   not important   a mystery   easy to explain

Write About It

What do you think happened to the *Cyclops*? Write a short paragraph, explaining your idea.

Focus on Vocabulary — Find the Meaning

Read each sentence. Circle the best meaning for the word or words in dark print.

1. People were surprised that a ship could just **vanish**.

   stop moving   disappear   turn around

2. The *Cyclops* disappeared in the **Bermuda Triangle**.

   area of the Atlantic Ocean   huge wave   strong storm

3. The **boundaries** run from Florida to Bermuda to Puerto Rico.

   lines marking an area's edges   telephone lines   beaches

4. The ship never sent an **S.O.S.**

   friendly message   good worker   call for help

5. Navy **officials** sent people to look for the ship.

   people in command   family members   enemy soldiers

6. Some people thought the ship struck a **mine**.

   hidden bomb   large rock   kind of fish

7. It was proven that no **torpedo** hit the ship.

   exploding rocket   rainstorm   small motor boat

8. No German **submarines** were in the area.

   airplanes   underwater ships   islands

9. One **theory** is that the captain was to blame.

   lie   idea   fact

10. The case is one of the most **baffling** ever.

    boring   hard to explain   famous

Map Keys

Maps use different symbols or colors. A **map key** tells what the symbols or colors mean. This map shows the Bermuda Triangle, where the U.S.S. *Cyclops* disappeared. Study the map and map key. Write the answer to each question below.

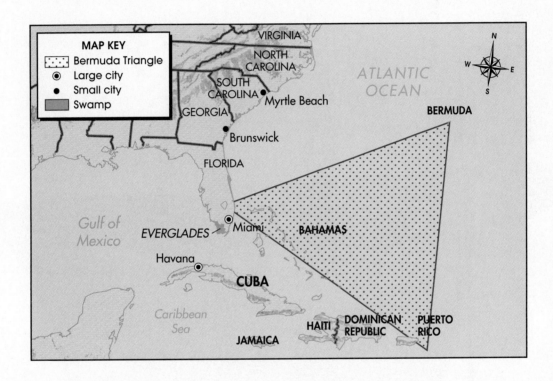

1. Draw the symbol for large city. _____

2. Is the symbol for river shown in the map key? _____

3. Is Miami a large city or a small city? _____

4. What two small cities are shown on the map? _____

_____

5. What swamp is shown on the map? _____

6. Are any islands of the Bahamas in the Bermuda Triangle? _____

101 Days at Sea

Thor Heyerdahl took one last look back at the South American coast on April 28, 1947. He could still see the country of Peru in the distance. If everything went well, Heyerdahl would not see land again for months. Instead, he would sail 4,300 miles across the South Pacific Ocean. Many others had made this trip. But they had done it in ships. Heyerdahl was trying to do it on a **raft**.

Drifting on the Ocean

Heyerdahl was trying to prove a theory. He believed that the islands in the South Pacific Ocean had been settled 1,500 years ago by people from a **civilization** in Peru. Scientists did not agree. They thought that the **islanders** had come from Asia.

Heyerdahl pointed out that long ago, sweet potatoes grew only in Peru. Yet somehow these vegetables also ended up growing in the South Pacific islands. The **ancient** Peruvians called their sweet potatoes "kumara." The South Pacific islanders used the same name for sweet potatoes. Also, the ancient Peruvians believed in a god they called "Kon-Tiki." The islanders called one of their gods "Tiki."

There seemed to be one big problem with Heyerdahl's theory, however. Ancient Peruvians had no ships. They used rafts made out of very light **balsa** wood. Such rafts could never have made it across the Pacific Ocean.

Or could they have? Heyerdahl wanted to find out. So he built a 45-foot balsa wood raft. He used the same materials that the ancient Peruvians had used. In the middle of the raft, he built a **bamboo** cabin. Then Heyerdahl added a big sail to catch the wind. For steering, he used a long oar. Heyerdahl called his raft *Kon-Tiki*.

Heyerdahl asked five men to join him. On April 28, they left a **harbor** of Peru and set out across the Pacific Ocean. After a few days, a storm hit. It lasted for five days and five nights. Heyerdahl was surprised at how well the raft survived the storm. It was light enough to climb to the top of the highest waves. It was also light enough to float when water washed over it.

A Tiki statue from the South Pacific

Close Calls

Soon after the storm ended, Heyerdahl and his crew spotted something coming toward them through the water. Heyerdahl described it in his journal. He wrote, "A huge whale headed directly at us, snorting like a galloping horse." When the whale was just six feet from the raft, it finally dived down under the water. The men could see it, **lurking** right below them. At last, they saw it "slowly sink deeper and deeper into the sea."

On May 10, the men got another scare. This time the trouble came from a shark. Crewman Herman Watzinger was trying to fix a loose log on the bottom of the raft. He paused to rest on the raft, his feet in the water. Suddenly, a brown shark slid through the waves. It swam right toward Watzinger.

Heyerdahl picked up a **harpoon**. He threw it at the shark. The harpoon hit the shark's back. Yet the creature kept coming. The men on the raft picked up a second harpoon. They used it to beat the shark over the head. At last, they drove the shark away. Watzinger stayed on the raft. He decided he wouldn't fix the log after all.

The *Kon-Tiki*'s crew were the first people to see the rare snake mackeral alive.

Adventures at Night

Night held its own adventures for the men on the *Kon-Tiki*. The crew slept in the bamboo cabin. The breeze blew in through the open windows. One night something else came in, as well. Torstein Raaby woke up to find a huge snake-like fish flopping around next to his ears. The creature was three feet long. It had a large mouth and "long, knife-sharp teeth."

Raaby didn't know it, but the long creature was a rare fish called a snake mackerel. People had thought this fish lived only at the bottom of the ocean. Said Heyerdahl, "It appeared later that we six sitting round the lamp in the bamboo cabin were the first men to have seen this fish alive."

The snake mackerel was not the only sea animal to make its way onto the *Kon-Tiki*. Flying fish often flew into the cabin. Once a dolphin jumped onto the raft. Even a baby octopus crawled on board.

The octopus worried the men the most. If a small one could make it onto the raft, so could a big one.

Thor Heyerdahl

A grown octopus is a dangerous creature. It has arms that are strong enough to kill a shark. Heyerdahl and his men could picture its "cold arms round our necks, dragging us out of our sleeping bags at night." The men began to sleep with knives in their hands, just in case.

Luckily, large octopuses never climbed onto the *Kon-Tiki*. And while the men had many adventures at sea, they also had many pleasant days. "Life is comfortable," wrote Heyerdahl one day. "We pass the time reading and studying. The amount of fish life around us is amazing.... We can catch more fish in five minutes than we can eat in two days."

On July 30, the six men at last saw land in the distance. Eight days later, they landed at Raroia Reef near the Tuamotu **Archipelago**, a group of islands in the South Pacific. Heyerdahl had proved his point that ancient Peruvians could have made the same voyage 1,500 years ago. It was possible to sail a balsa wood raft across the Pacific Ocean and live to tell the tale.

The *Kon-Tiki*'s crew reached the South Pacific after 101 days at sea.

Read and Remember — Check the Events

Place a check in front of the three sentences that tell what happened in the story.

_____ **1.** Thor Heyerdahl grew up on a South Pacific island.

_____ **2.** The *Kon-Tiki* sank during a bad storm.

_____ **3.** Thor Heyerdahl sailed a raft from Peru to the South Pacific.

_____ **4.** Sharks killed two of Heyerdahl's men.

_____ **5.** Many sea creatures climbed onto the *Kon-Tiki*.

_____ **6.** It took 101 days for the *Kon-Tiki* to reach Raroia Reef.

Think About It — Drawing Conclusions

Write one or more sentences to answer each question.

1. Why did Thor Heyerdahl think people from the South Pacific islands came from Peru? _____

_____

2. Why did Heyerdahl use the same materials for his raft as the ancient Peruvians had used for their rafts? _____

_____

3. What made Herman Watzinger decide not to fix the log on the bottom of the raft? _____

_____

4. Why was it exciting that the men found a snake mackeral? _____

_____

5. Why were the men worried about an octopus climbing onto the raft?

_____

Focus on Vocabulary — Match Up

Match each word with its meaning. Write the correct letter on the blank.

_____ **1.** raft

_____ **2.** balsa

_____ **3.** islanders

_____ **4.** harpoon

_____ **5.** civilization

_____ **6.** ancient

_____ **7.** archipelago

_____ **8.** bamboo

_____ **9.** lurking

_____ **10.** harbor

a. a kind of wood that is light but strong

b. from a long time ago

c. long, sharp weapon connected to a rope

d. a sheltered place where ships can stay

e. a group of islands

f. a kind of flat boat made from pieces of wood

g. a place where people live and share customs

h. moving or waiting in a sneaky way

i. people who live on islands

j. tall grass that looks like tubes of thin wood

Countries

Some maps give information about countries. The map key explains what symbols are used on the map. The map below shows Peru, from where Thor Heyerdahl sailed. It also shows the countries that are on Peru's **borders**. Study the map and the map key. Write the answer to each question.

1. What is the capital city of Peru? _____

2. What other cities in Peru are shown on the map? _____

3. In which country is Quito the capital city? _____

4. Name the five countries that share a border with Peru. _____

5. What mountains are shown on the map? _____

6. Does the equator run through Ecuador? _____

Without Warning

standing on the deck of the *Albatross*, Dr. Christopher Sheldon saw small flashes of lightning. He wasn't worried that a storm might be coming. He and his crew actually hoped the storm's wind would help their 92-foot sailboat pick up speed as it crossed the **Gulf** of Mexico. But the storm that hit the *Albatross* on May 2, 1961, was stronger than anyone expected. In fact, for six people on board, it proved to be deadly.

A Morning at Sea

Christopher Sheldon's *Albatross* was more than a ship. It was a "floating classroom." Sheldon had set up a school on board. He called it the "Ocean Academy." Sheldon was both **skipper** and head teacher. His wife, Dr. Alice Sheldon, was the ship's doctor and science teacher. The Sheldons also hired a math teacher, an English teacher, and a cook. Then they looked for 14 teenage boys with a sense of adventure for the sea. These boys became students and crewmen on the *Albatross*.

In 1960 the Sheldons, teachers, and students set sail from Bermuda, an island in the Atlantic Ocean. During the eight-month voyage, the boys had to do school work. But they also learned how to sail. The Sheldons believed that the experiences of life at sea helped teenagers grow into strong adults.

The group sailed on the *Albatross* down to the Panama **Canal**. Then they headed out across the Pacific Ocean. They explored the Galápagos Islands off the coast of South America.

The Sheldons thought of the Ocean Academy as a "floating classroom."

By May 1961, the group had traveled north to Mexico. They had been sailing for seven months. At last, they were going home to the United States. The *Albatross* headed out across the Gulf of Mexico.

On the morning of May 2, everyone ate breakfast as usual. A few raindrops fell on the deck of the *Albatross*. There was no wind at all. After breakfast, the crew and teachers began their daily tasks.

No Warning

Suddenly, around 9 A.M., a **violent** storm hit the *Albatross*. Within seconds, the sea became an angry swirl of waves. Cold rain poured from the sky. Wind ripped at the ship's sails.

The boys had never seen anything like it before. But Christopher Sheldon knew what it was. It was a deadly **white squall**. This rare storm strikes without warning. It brings no storm clouds. Instead, it brings rain and **terrifying** blasts of wind.

The wind caught hold of the sails of the *Albatross*. English teacher Richard Langford later explained what happened. The wind pressed the ship sideways "down into the sea, the way a **hurricane** bends a tree to the ground. Her huge sails filled with tons of seawater, and she couldn't rise." In just 60 seconds, the *Albatross* sank into the Gulf of Mexico, never to be seen again.

When the *Albatross* **capsized**, the people below deck were trapped in the ship. "Water was rushing in very fast," said student Tim Barrows. Some of the boys were able to push their way up a ladder against the rushing water. Another boy crashed through a door to escape. Langford and teacher John Perry also made it out of the sinking ship. Three boys who were below deck did not.

Meanwhile, the skipper and crew on the deck above had been thrown into the sea. They splashed around wildly, gasping for air. Two of the boys knew that Dr. Alice and the cook were trapped in a room off the deck. The boys swam to that door and tried to pull it open. But the door wouldn't move. Dr. Alice and the cook both went down with the ship.

Into the Lifeboats

One other person lost his life in the storm. He was 18-year-old John Goodlett. Goodlett was the best swimmer on the *Albatross*. He struggled to cut a lifeboat free from the sinking ship. At last, he

A scene from the movie "White Squall" shows the *Albatross* during the sudden storm.

John Goodlett

succeeded. But the freed boat swung around and hit him in the head. Goodlett sank under the water.

As the lifeboat bobbed upside-down in the water, some of the boys clung to it. They knew Goodlett had died getting it for them. Said one of the students later, "he's the only reason any of us are alive."

A second lifeboat bobbed up from the sunken *Albatross*, so there was enough room for everyone. The skipper, two teachers, and ten boys survived the white squall. But their ship was gone, and they were miles from land. They knew that no one would be coming to help them because they hadn't had time to send an S.O.S.

The **survivors** were shocked by the death of Dr. Alice and the others. They didn't talk about it as they floated on the sea. But each of them was thinking of the friends they had just lost. As the hours passed, seven-foot sharks began circling the lifeboats. At last, two days later, a large ship passed by. It picked up everyone in the lifeboats.

The group knew that they were lucky to be alive. Yet they could not forget those who had died. One of the students said years later, "The image of my friends lying a mile and a half deep at the bottom of the ocean has stayed with me. There was no time to say goodbye."

Rescued at last, the survivors were glad to finally see land.

USE WHAT YOU KNOW

Read and Remember — Finish the Sentence

Circle the best ending for each sentence.

1. The Sheldons thought of the *Albatross* as a "floating _____."
   hospital   hotel   classroom

2. In May 1961, the *Albatross* was sailing across the _____.
   Pacific Ocean   Gulf of Mexico   Indian Ocean

3. A sudden storm caused the sailboat to _____.
   tip over   hit rocks   hit another ship

4. Some of the boys were trapped _____.
   below deck   on shore   in a lifeboat

5. John Goodlett lost his life while cutting loose _____.
   a fish   an anchor   a lifeboat

Write About It

Imagine you were one of the boys from the *Albatross*. Write a short paragraph telling why you wanted to join the Sheldons' Ocean Academy.

USE WHAT YOU KNOW

Focus on Vocabulary — Find the Meaning

Read each sentence. Circle the best meaning for the word or words in dark print.

1. The *Albatross* sailed through the Panama **Canal**.

    jungles   dangerous land   river made by people

2. During the storm, the *Albatross* **capsized**.

    turned upside-down   slowed down   became lost

3. The *Albatross* was hit by a **white squall**.

    strange fish   enemy boat   deadly storm at sea

4. Christopher Sheldon was the sailboat's **skipper**.

    captain   cook   guide

5. It reminded Richard Langford of a **hurricane**.

    strong, windy rainstorm   bad flood   dark tunnel

6. Some boys **succeeded** in getting out alive.

    completed as desired   gave up hope   helped others

7. The **survivors** were shocked by the death of Dr. Alice.

    doctors   people who lived   rescue workers

8. The storm brought **terrifying** blasts of wind.

    fresh and light   very scary   slow and steady

9. The sailboat crossed the **Gulf** of Mexico.

    water near a bend of land   ring of islands   border

10. The **violent** storm hit the *Albatross* at about 9 A.M.

    slow-moving   powerful   quiet

Distance Scale

On a map, we use a **distance scale** to find the distance between two places. This map shows Central America, which the *Albatross* sailed past during part of its voyage. The map's distance scale shows that 1 inch stands for 200 miles of land. Use a ruler to measure the distances on the map. Circle the correct answer to each question.

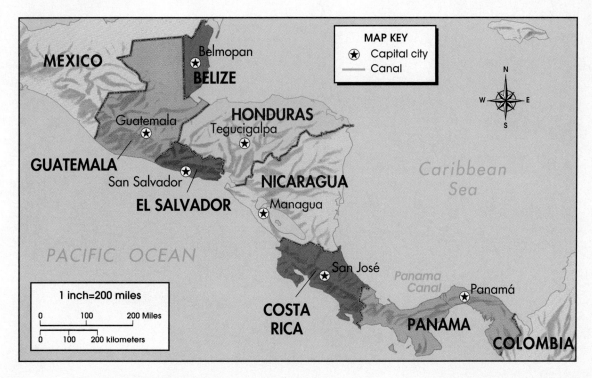

1. How many inches are between Guatemala and San Salvador on the map?

    2 inches $1\frac{1}{2}$ inches $\frac{1}{2}$ inch

2. What is the actual distance between Guatemala and San Salvador?

    50 miles   100 miles   200 miles

3. What is the actual distance between San José and the Panama Canal?

    400 miles   250 miles   500 miles

4. Which city is 150 miles from Tegucigalpa?

    Guatemala   Managua   Belmopan

Shark Attack!

R odney Fox swam down deeper into the water. He could see a fish hiding in the seaweed below him. When he got close enough, he planned to **spear** the fish.

Fox was taking part in a spearfishing contest near Aldinga Beach in South Australia. Many people were in this contest in the Indian Ocean. At the end of the day, everyone else would go home. But Rodney Fox would end up in a hospital, fighting for his life.

Great White Sharks

Rodney Fox loved to swim and to go spearfishing. He would hold his breath and dive down. Then he would drift through the water with his **speargun** in one hand. A weighted belt around his waist kept him from bobbing up to the surface. The belt was tied to a marker that floated in the waves.

On December 8, 1963, Fox was about to spear a fish for the contest when suddenly he felt that something wasn't right. Before he could move, a creature slammed into him from behind. He felt dozens of sharp teeth sinking into his chest and back. "I knew **immediately** that it was a shark," Fox later said.

The shark that grabbed onto Fox was not just any shark. It was a terrifying Great White. These sharks can be found near the coasts of many **regions** of the world, especially near Australia and South Africa. Most adult Great White sharks are 12–16 feet long. They have row after row of pointed teeth. These teeth are so sharp that they can saw through wood.

Many people go spearfishing in waters where sharks are present.

A Great White shark kills by biting into its **victim** hard. As the victim begins to bleed, the shark moves in and begins feeding. Great White sharks can make a meal out of an 800-pound elephant seal. So killing a human isn't difficult. Ten to 15 people are killed each year by Great White sharks. Now it looked as though Rodney Fox was about to add to that number.

A Struggle Begins

When Fox felt the shark bite him, fear flooded his body. He dropped his speargun. Yet he was still able to think. "A friend of mine had been attacked by a shark, and we had discussed it many times," he later said. Brian Rodgers had told Fox that he should punch an attacking shark in the eye. That was one spot where sharks could be hurt.

Fox reached around with his right arm. He hoped to hit the shark's eye. But right at that moment, the creature let go of him. Fox **plunged** his arm into the shark's mouth by mistake. By the time Fox pulled it out, his arm and hand were torn to pieces.

Fox struggled to the surface. He took a big breath of air. Blood poured from his body. The water around him was turning red. Still, the water was clear enough for Fox to see the shark coming toward him again. Its mouth was open. Its teeth were bared. "I thought I was gone," Fox remembered.

As the shark closed in on him, Fox kicked out his leg. He tried to knock the creature away. He hoped it would take his foot or his leg and leave the rest of him alone. Fox did manage to push the shark off course. But as it rushed past him, its teeth caught the rope attached to Fox's belt. The shark swallowed the rope. Then it swam off into deeper water, dragging Fox along.

Fighting for His Life

Fox was pulled through the seawater at high speed. He twisted around and around at the end of the rope. Blood continued to flow from his body. He felt his lungs running out of air. Fox could not use his torn right hand. But with his left hand, he reached down to his weight belt. He tried to unhook the belt. He couldn't do it. The buckle had been pulled around to the back.

Just as Fox was about to give up and breathe in water, he felt the rope snap. The shark had bitten right

Rodney Fox

Rodney Fox got 462 stitches in his left side and arm after the shark attack.

Today, divers use special cages to study Great White sharks.

through it. That gave Fox fresh hope. Somehow he held his breath just a little longer. His body floated up to the surface. There he gasped for air and began to scream for help. Divers in nearby boats quickly scooped Fox up and headed for shore.

Fox was having trouble breathing. His right arm and hand were in shreds. His ribs were crushed. So was his left lung. In fact, his body was cut almost in half. He was held together only by his **wet suit**.

The hospital was 38 miles away. It was a rough trip. Fox struggled to stay alive. Fox's friend Malcolm Baker sat beside him the whole way. Baker kept shouting, "Keep trying, Rodney, keep fighting!"

Said Fox, "Just breathing was the hardest thing I can ever remember."

Surgeons spent hours putting Fox's body back together. They put 462 **stitches** in his left side. They put another 92 in his right hand.

Yet Fox survived. He was covered in **scars**. Three months later, he was back in the water again. In fact, he soon took a new job as a diver. Often he was asked how he dared go into the water after that terrible day. "You have to live with sharks as they are," Fox said. "You can't go around being afraid of them...." Then he added, "To allow fear of them to keep you from the sea is to miss out on one of the greatest things in life."

Read and Remember — Choose the Answer

Draw a circle around the correct answer.

1. What was Rodney Fox doing when he was attacked?
   resting on a float   spearfishing   steering a boat

2. Where was Fox when the shark attacked him?
   Australia   South America   Europe

3. What part of the shark did Fox try to punch?
   the tail   the stomach   the eye

4. What did the shark swallow?
   a rope   a speargun   a boat

5. What did surgeons give Fox at the hospital?
   a new lung   an arm made of plastic   462 stitches

6. After the attack, what job did Fox take?
   diver   hospital worker   fisherman

Think About It — Find the Sequence

Number the sentences to show the correct order from the story. The first one is done for you.

_____ 1. A shark slammed into Fox from behind.

__1__ 2. Rodney Fox entered a contest near Aldinga Beach.

_____ 3. Fox put his arm into the shark's mouth by mistake.

_____ 4. Fox took a new job as a diver.

_____ 5. The shark bit through the rope that was tied to Fox's belt.

_____ 6. Friends rushed Fox to the hospital.

Focus on Vocabulary — Make a Word

Choose a word in dark print to complete each sentence. Write the letters of the word on the blanks. When you are finished, the letters in the circles will tell you what kind of shark attacked Rodney Fox.

speargun	**immediately**	**plunged**	**surgeons**
regions	**victim**	**wet suit**	**spear**
stitches	**scars**		

1. Rodney Fox _____ his arm into the shark's mouth.

○ _ _ _ _ _ _ _

2. _____ had to sew Fox back together.

○ _ _ _ _ _ _ _ _

3. Fox was about to _____ a fish.

○ _ _ _ _ _

4. After the attack, Fox was covered with _____.

○ _ _ _ _ _

5. Fox was the _____ of a shark attack.

○ _ _ _ _ _ _

6. Fox was held together by his _____.

○ _ _ _ _ _ _ _ _

7. Fox had 92 _____ in his right hand.

○ _ _ _ _ _ _ _ _

8. Sharks live in many different _____ of the world.

○ _ _ _ _ _ _ _

9. Fox knew _____ what was happening.

○ _ _ _ _ _ _ _ _ _ _ _

10. Fox dropped the _____ he was holding.

○ _ _ _ _ _ _ _ _

Latitude and Longitude

Lines that run east to west around Earth are lines of **latitude**. Lines that run north to south are lines of **longitude**. All the lines are measured in **degrees**, or °. Latitude and longitude can be used to show a place's location. For example, the city of Adelaide, Australia, is at 34°S, 138°E. The latitude is written first, then the longitude. Study the map of Australia below. Circle the answer that best completes each sentence.

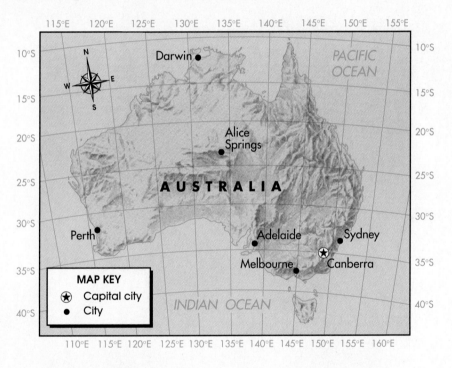

1. The city that has a latitude of 12°S is _____.

   Perth   Alice Springs   Darwin

2. The city that has a longitude of 116°E is _____.

   Sydney   Melbourne   Perth

3. The latitude of Canberra, the capital city, is _____.

   35°S   25°S   148°E

4. The city at 38°S, 145°E is _____.

   Sydney   Melbourne   Perth

A Dangerous Swim

Diana Nyad wanted to be the first person ever to swim from Cuba to Florida. That is a distance of 103 miles across the Straits of Florida. No person had swum that far in the open sea. Nyad knew it would be the hardest thing she had ever done. She called it her "own private **Olympics**." She had spent a long time training for the swim. Still, as she stood on Cuba's north coast, she was scared. Could she make it? "If anyone can do it, I can," said Nyad bravely.

A Strong Swimmer

Nyad had been been training to be a champion swimmer since she was a child. She wanted to be on the 1968 United States Olympic swim team. But during try-outs, Nyad had a problem. There was an **infection** in her heart. The infection didn't last, but it was enough to keep her off the team. Her dream of going to the Olympics was over.

After that, Nyad turned to **marathon** swimming. In this sport, people swim long distances. Nyad swam 22 miles in Africa's Nile River. She also swam 32 miles across Lake Ontario in North America. Nyad even swam around Manhattan Island in New York City. She covered those 28 miles in just less than 8 hours.

The swim between Cuba and Florida would be much harder than any of these, however. She expected that it would take her about sixty hours.

Nyad's plan was simple enough. She would swim north to the **Gulf Stream**. This ocean current would help carry her east. When she reached the other side

Nyad swam inside a cage attached to a boat.

of the Gulf Stream, she would be near Florida. She hoped to end her swim in the group of islands called the Florida **Keys**.

Nyad planned to make her swim in the summer of 1978. July would be the best month. The sea is calm at that time of the year. Also, the winds are light. But the starting date was **delayed**. Cuban officials took a long time before they allowed her into the country.

Bad Weather

At last, on August 13, Diana Nyad stood on Cuba's Ortegosa Beach, about 50 miles west of Havana, the **capital city** of Cuba. Nyad was ready to begin. But the season was changing. The water would be rougher now. The winds would be stronger. But Nyad didn't care. She had trained too long and too hard to turn back. At 2:07 P.M. she waded into the sea.

Nyad was not alone on her swim. A boat sailed next to her. Its crew had food and fresh water ready to hand to her. The crew was also there to cheer her on.

Nyad swam inside a big cage. It was 40 feet long and 21 feet wide. The cage let the water through but kept out sharks.

But things did not work out the way Diana Nyad had planned. Strong winds began to kick up waves. That caused her cage to rock. Worse, the cage itself made waves. So Nyad had to swim through water that was always **churning**. The rough waves tossed her from side to side.

Trying to help, Nyad's crew changed her course slightly. But the wind kept blowing hard. Soon Nyad became **seasick**. She threw up many times. That, in turn, made her weaker and more tired.

As the hours went by, other problems occurred. The cage kept out the sharks. But it didn't keep out the jellyfish. Again and again they stung Nyad's arms and legs, making her scream in pain. The saltwater caused her lips and tongue to swell. The temperature of the sea was a warm 85 **degrees**. But Nyad shivered whenever she stopped swimming, even for a moment. By 2 A.M. the next morning, her body temperature began to drop. "This is the worst night of my life," Nyad cried. But she kept going.

A jellyfish

Swimming in Circles

As the sun rose, Nyad felt a little better. She was able to eat a little food. Once again, she began to swim strongly. Still, she sensed that something was wrong. She didn't know it, but she was heading more to the west, away from Florida. "Can we reach Florida in 60 hours?" she asked a crew member. "Yes," she was told, "it's still possible." Nyad continued to swim. But she wondered whether she could really make it to Florida.

Then another crew member told Nyad something she didn't want to hear. "Diana, you've done 53 miles." Perhaps the person was trying to make Nyad feel better. But from Nyad's point of view, it was bad news. It meant she hadn't even gone halfway.

She swam on through the second night. By the next morning, the sea was rough again. Then the crew discovered that they were way off course. Crew member Rich du Moulin gave Nyad the bad news. "You've been swimming in circles," he told her. "There's no way you're going to reach Florida.... It's time to call it quits."

Nyad was terribly disappointed. But she had no choice. Nyad had swum 76 miles in 42 hours. But she was only 50 miles from where she started. That left another 53 miles to go. "I've never been so tired in my life," Nyad said with tears in her eyes. "I'm feeling pains I've never felt before." With that, she climbed into the boat and rode the rest of the way to Florida.

Nyad had not completed her amazing swim. But there was no doubt that Diana Nyad had shown the world that she was a champion.

Nyad was glad her long swim was over.

Read and Remember — Check the Events

Place a check in front of the three sentences that tell what happened in the story.

_____ **1.** Diana Nyad refused to swim in Africa's Nile River.

_____ **2.** Nyad swam inside a big cage to keep out sharks.

_____ **3.** During her swim, Nyad was stung by jellyfish.

_____ **4.** Nyad decided to swim all the way to New Jersey.

_____ **5.** For many hours, Nyad swam in circles.

_____ **6.** After her swim, Nyad realized she had lost her hearing.

Write About It

Imagine you were a newspaper reporter in 1978. You are about to interview Diana Nyad. Write three questions that you would like to ask her.

1. _____

   _____

2. _____

   _____

3. _____

   _____

Focus on Vocabulary — Match Up

Match each word with its meaning. Write the correct letter on the blank.

_____ **1.** keys

_____ **2.** capital city

_____ **3.** churning

_____ **4.** Gulf Stream

_____ **5.** delayed

_____ **6.** degrees

_____ **7.** seasick

_____ **8.** Olympics

_____ **9.** marathon

_____ **10.** infection

a. main city of the government of a state or country

b. disease that is spread by a germ

c. very long race

d. units of measure for temperature

e. warm water of the Atlantic Ocean flowing east past Florida

f. put off until later

g. small, low islands near shore

h. feeling ill because of waves

i. sports contests between different countries

j. stirring up

Route Map

A **route map** shows the roads and highways in an area. The map key shows the symbols used for different kinds of roads and highways. This route map is of southern Florida and the Florida Keys, to which Diana Nyad tried to swim. Study the map and the map key. Write the answer to each question.

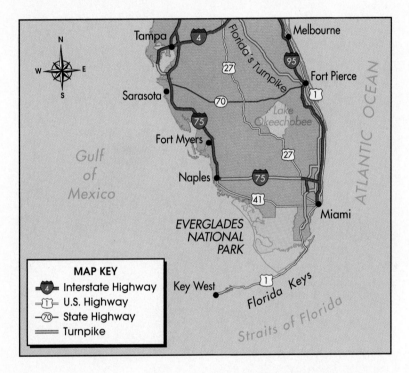

1. Which U.S. highway could you take to get from Miami to Lake Okeechobee? _____

2. Which kind of highway goes along the Florida Keys? _____

3. Which two interstate highways meet near Tampa? _____

4. Which state highway could you take to get from Fort Pierce to Sarasota? _____

5. Which U.S. highway could you take to get from Naples to the Everglades National Park? _____

Whales in Trouble

The hunters from Yandrakinot could barely believe their eyes. They had heard that whales were swimming near their village in northeast Russia. Now their families would have plenty of food for the long winter ahead. Happily, the hunters rushed down to the water. But their happiness soon turned to worry. There were not just a few whales. There were thousands of them. Something was terribly wrong.

Trapped by the Ice

The whales the men saw were **belugas**. These beautiful white whales are perfectly suited to life in cold water. They live in and around the **Arctic Circle**. Belugas can easily find their way around the blocks of ice that often dot the water. But in December of 1984, there was a lot more ice than usual.

During that month, the belugas came into a narrow strip of water called the Senyavina Strait. The strait is near the Bering Sea between Russia and Alaska. The belugas were chasing cod, a kind of fish they liked to eat. But slowly, a strong east wind began to blow. The wind blew huge chunks of ice called **floes** into the strait. The chunks got pushed together, forming **pack ice**. This ice soon blocked the strait.

The belugas didn't notice what was happening. They were too busy feasting on cod. By the time they turned to leave the strait, it was too late. The pack ice had become a huge wall. It measured 18 miles long, 11 miles wide, and 12 feet thick.

There was no way the belugas could push through the ice. They couldn't swim under it, either. They were trapped. Three thousand belugas now struggled to find air holes in the pack ice. They did find some small pools of open water. The whales crowded around these. They had to take turns breathing. Mothers struggled to push their babies up through the crowd to get air.

The people of Yandrakinot were **horrified**. Day after day they watched to see if the ice would break up. But it only got thicker. Every day the trapped whales grew weaker. The people went to their homes and pulled out fish they had frozen for the winter. They brought it down to the water and threw it to the trapped whales. But they knew it was not enough. Unless someone else came to the rescue, the whales would die.

Help on the Way

On January 29, 1985, word of the trapped whales reached the government in the city of Moscow. Officials flew to Senyavina Strait. They knew the ice had to be broken apart to save the whales. So they called Anatoly Kovalenko. He was the captain of a huge ship named the *Moskva*. The *Moskva* was an

The pack ice trapped the whales in the strait.

To reach the whales, an icebreaker had to cut through the pack ice.

icebreaker. Its job was to lead other boats through icy waters. So it was built to plow through ice.

On February 7, the *Moskva* headed for the strait. Captain Kovalenko hoped to cut a path through the ice. Then the whales could swim to freedom.

As he neared the pack ice, Kovalenko became very worried. The ice was **shifting** all the time. The front of the icebreaker could cut through it. But if some of the big chunks squeezed the sides of the *Moskva*, the ship could be crushed to pieces. Twice, Kovalenko turned around and headed back out of the strait.

But by now, the whales were in bad shape. About 40 had already died. The rest were growing weaker by the hour. Kovalenko knew he had to try again.

So for the third time, the *Moskva* pushed slowly through the ice. Planes flew overhead to guide the ship. People around the world waited to find out if the icebreaker could get through. They called the rescue effort "**Operation** Beluga."

Music for the Whales

At last, on February 22 the *Moskva* reached the whales. The ship had cut a path that would take the belugas back to the open ocean. If the belugas would follow the *Moskva*, they would be safe. But the whales were scared of the big ship. They didn't like its noisy engines. They tried to hide from it.

For four days the *Moskva* stayed near the belugas. Kovalenko hoped the belugas would get used to the sight and sound of his ship. While he waited, he made the pools of open water bigger. That allowed the whales to breathe more easily. As the days passed, the belugas grew stronger and more **active**. At last, he said, "they began to approach the boat... and leaped like children."

But the whales would not follow the ship out to open water. The crew of the *Moskva* didn't know what to do. At last, one man remembered that dolphins like music. Perhaps whales would, too. Kovalenko ordered loud music to be played from the deck. He tried all different kinds. The whales seemed to like **classical** music. When they heard the music, they began to follow the ship.

People cheered as Captain Kovalenko led the belugas out of Senyavina Strait. By February 26, the whales were safely out in the open ocean again. Operation Beluga was a great success.

At last, the belugas were safe in the open ocean.

USE WHAT YOU KNOW

Read and Remember — Finish the Sentence

Circle the best ending for each sentence.

1. The whales became trapped when they were chasing _____.

    fish   ships   hunters

2. The trapped whales gathered around small _____.

    air holes   boats   fishing nets

3. The *Moskva* was built to break through _____.

    wood   rock   ice

4. To free the whales, the *Moskva* had to cut a path to _____.

    the open sea   the Indian Ocean   Moscow

5. The whales followed the ship when they heard _____.

    thunder   human voices   music

Think About It — Cause and Effect

A **cause** is something that makes something else happen. What happens is called the **effect**. Match each cause with an effect. Write the letter on the correct blank. The first one is done for you.

Cause	Effect
1. The whales wanted to eat cod, so __c__	**a.** they would not follow the ship.
2. Senyavina Strait became jammed with ice, so _____	**b.** the whales could not leave.
3. The people of Yandrakinot wanted to help, so _____	**c.** they followed the fish into Senyavina Strait.
4. The whales were afraid of the *Moskva*, so _____	**d.** they threw frozen fish to the whales.

Focus on Vocabulary — Finish Up

Choose the correct word or words in dark print to complete each sentence.

Arctic Circle   **pack ice**   **operation**   **icebreaker**
floes   **horrified**   **classical**   **shifting**
belugas   **active**

1. To be shocked and upset is to be _____.

2. Large chunks of ice in the water are called _____.

3. A ship built to cut through ice is called an _____.

4. White whales that live in cold waters are _____.

5. Blocks of ice that get jammed together form _____.

6. Music that has no words and follows certain rules is _____ music.

7. To move your body around is to be _____.

8. When something is changing its position, it is _____ around.

9. The imaginary line that goes around the region near the North Pole is the _____.

10. An action planned out ahead of time is an _____.

Elevation

An area of land can have different **elevations**, or heights. Some areas have low plains. Other areas have tall mountains. The map below uses colors to show different elevations of the land around the Bering Strait, near where the belugas were trapped. The map key shows which color is used for certain heights. Study the map and the map key. Circle the best answer to each question.

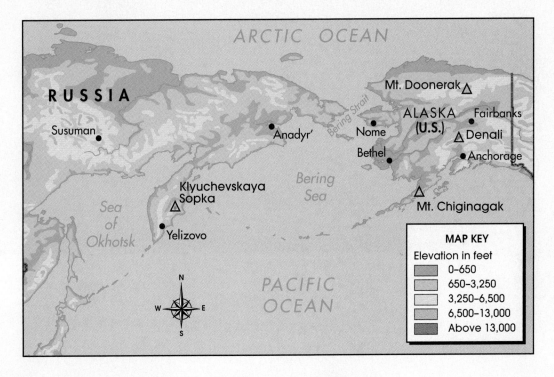

1. Which color shows the highest elevation?

   dark orange   yellow   dark green

2. What is the elevation of the city of Susuman in Russia?

   0–650 feet   3,250–6,500 feet   above 13,000 feet

3. Which mountain peak is at the highest elevation?

   Mount Doonerck   Denali   Mount Chiginagak

4. Which city is at the lowest elevation?

   Bethel   Fairbanks   Yelizovo

Lucky to Be Alive

Margaret Crotty looked forward to a quiet weekend. She had a busy job helping children in Indonesia, a country in Asia. So the 23-year-old American woman decided to spend a few days on the island of Weh. This Indonesian island is known for its lovely beaches. On January 19, 1996, Crotty climbed onto the **ferryboat** *Gurita*. The boat then headed across the Andaman Sea. It was supposed to reach Weh in a little over two hours. But it never made it.

Death in the Water

At first, it was a happy voyage. Many of the 377 people on board were going to Weh to visit family and friends. The boat was very crowded. In fact, the *Gurita* had far too many people on board. The ferry was also carrying a large load of heavy **concrete**. It wasn't built to carry so much weight. Yet the old ferry sailed on for two hours.

Then, half an hour from Weh, the *Gurita* sprang a leak. The ferry began to rock wildly in the rough seas. Screaming people slid from one side of the boat to the other. The ferry began to sink. Soon it flipped over on its side. People fell into the sea. Many people drowned because they couldn't swim.

Margaret Crotty tried to keep calm. She saw that no one was wearing a life jacket. So she ran to a bin and began to hand them out. There weren't enough life jackets for everyone. Crotty didn't even save one for herself. Still, she stayed calm. She was a great swimmer. She had been a **lifeguard** as a teenager.

Margaret Crotty wanted to relax on the beaches of an Indonesian island.

Besides, Crotty felt sure that help must be on the way. She had no idea that she would spend the next 16 hours swimming for her life.

A Lifeguard Trick

Just as Crotty was about to move away from the bin, the boat shifted. The **jolt** sent her tumbling into the bin. The lid slammed shut. Crotty was trapped inside. Water began to rush in. Soon, her head was underwater. She began to swallow water. "This is it," she thought. "This is what it's like to die."

Luckily, the lid hadn't locked. Crotty gave it one last **desperate** kick. It sprang open and she swam out. A moment later she popped to the surface of the sea. Crotty had escaped death by a few seconds.

It was now about 8:30 P.M. Against the dark sky, Crotty could see a rubber raft with lots of people on it. There were no other rafts in sight. Crotty swam over to the raft but did not get on. The raft was already too full. Part of it began to leak and sink. Some of the people fell off. Once again, those who couldn't swim drowned.

Crotty now saw that help might not come any time soon. Luckily, she remembered an old trick she had learned as a lifeguard. Crotty took off her pants and tied the two legs together. Then she blew air into the pants. That made a kind of balloon. She trapped the air by pulling the string at the waist. Crotty's little balloon helped to keep her **afloat**.

Hanging On

As Crotty bobbed in the water, she felt a pain in her left leg. Looking down, she saw a deep cut in her ankle. She was bleeding. She had cut herself while kicking open the life jacket bin. A sudden fear gripped her. These waters were filled with sharks. What if her blood **attracted** them? "Now I was truly afraid," she later wrote. Luckily, no sharks came near her.

Hours passed. Crotty kept drifting west across the Andaman Sea. Strong ocean currents took her 30 miles from the wreck. Crotty began to think about home and how awful it would be to die so young. She knew that she had to keep going. "If you can last until dawn, someone will see you, and you will be rescued," Crotty told herself.

The struggle to stay afloat had worn her out. Yet somehow she managed to stay alive. At dawn, the sea grew rougher. The huge waves made it impossible for her to float on her back. By now, she had been in the water for 14 hours.

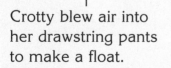

Crotty blew air into her drawstring pants to make a float.

Then she saw something floating in the water. It was a man! He, too, came from the *Gurita*. He was wearing a life jacket and holding onto a seat cushion. Crotty called out to the man. "I can't help you," he answered. "I can't swim."

"I know," Crotty said. "I'm just so glad to see someone else."

The man had some lollipops and offered her one. This gave her new **energy** and lifted her spirits. Soon, however, the currents carried the man away.

Once again, Crotty was alone. In the distance, she saw one island after another. But the currents kept sweeping her past them. At last, she spotted what she knew was the last island in this **chain**. If she missed it, she would see no other land for more than a thousand miles.

Gathering her last bit of strength, Margaret Crotty began swimming for the rocky **shoreline**. Somehow, she made it. As she lay on rocks, two boats arrived. They were looking for survivors. Gratefully, Crotty climbed into one. She was safe at last. The man who had floated by her also was rescued. Later, Crotty learned she was one of only 39 people to survive this terrifying night at sea. "I realized just how lucky I was," she said.

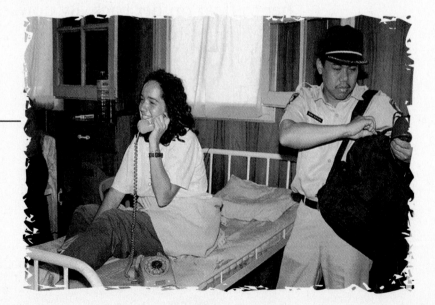

Crotty called her family from the hospital to let them know she was safe.

Read and Remember — Choose the Answer

Draw a circle around the correct answer.

1. What happened to the *Gurita*?

   It sank.   It got lost.   It was robbed.

2. What did Margaret Crotty hand out to people?

   tickets   food   life jackets

3. What did Crotty use to make a kind of balloon?

   her pants   a sail   sheets

4. What was one thing Crotty worried about?

   the sun   TV cameras   sharks

5. What was Crotty given by the man holding a seat cushion?

   money   a lollipop   directions

6. How did Crotty finally get to shore?

   by helicopter   by swimming   on a raft

Write About It

Imagine you are Margaret Crotty. Write a short paragraph, telling why it is a good idea to learn how to swim.

Focus on Vocabulary — Crossword Puzzle

Use the clues to complete the puzzle. Choose from the words in dark print.

energy	**attracted**	**concrete**	**ferryboat**
chain	**afloat**	**desperate**	**lifeguard**
shoreline	**jolt**		

Across

3. boat that takes people short distances

4. land along the edge of a sea

5. drew to oneself

8. mix of sand and cement

9. person hired to keep swimmers safe

Down

1. almost out of hope

2. sudden jerk or bump

5. floating

6. a series of related things, such as islands

7. strength to do work

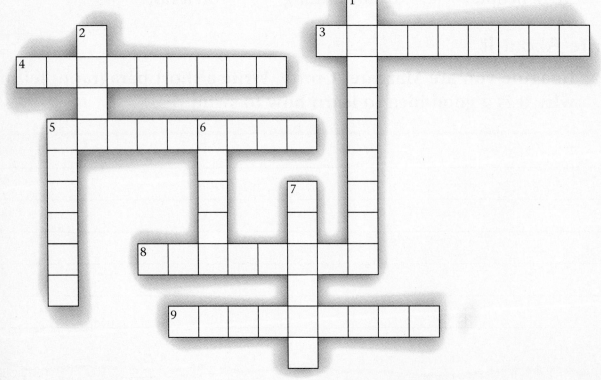

Countries

Some maps give information about countries. Thin lines are used to show the **borders** between countries. The map key explains what symbols are used on the map. This map shows Southeast Asia. The *Gurita* sank in the Andaman Sea in Southeast Asia. Study the map and the map key. Write the answer to each question.

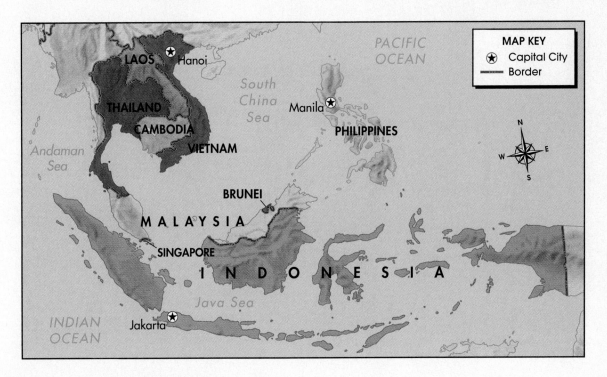

1. What is the capital city of Indonesia? _____

2. In which country is Hanoi the capital city? _____

3. Which three countries share a border with Cambodia? _____

_____

4. Which sea is just west of the Philippines? _____

5. Do Malaysia and Indonesia share a border? _____

6. Which country surrounds the Java Sea? _____

Escape to Freedom

Orlando Hernandez climbed onto the 20-foot wooden boat. He and his seven friends knew they might die. But they were desperate to escape Cuba, an island country along the Caribbean Sea. They wanted to be free from the Cuban government.

As Hernandez and the others pushed off from the shore on December 26, 1997, they wondered what would happen next. Would they make it to freedom? Or would they die at sea?

Cuban Baseball Hero

Orlando Hernandez was a hero. He was the best baseball pitcher in all of Cuba. His fans called him "El Duque," or "The Duke." Hernandez had won 129 games in his career while losing only 47. In 1992 he led the Cuban team to an Olympic gold medal.

In 1996 however, the Cuban government **banned** El Duque from baseball. He would never be allowed to pitch in Cuba again. He had to work in a hospital. His **salary** was only $8.75 a month.

What had Orlando done wrong? In truth, he had done nothing wrong. But the Cuban government thought he had.

In 1995 El Duque was visiting Mexico with the Cuban baseball team. Orlando's half brother, Livan Hernandez, was also on the team. Like Orlando, Livan was a great pitcher. But Livan was unhappy in Cuba. He wanted to move to the United States. The Cuban officials wouldn't let him, so Livan decided to **defect**, or run away. While he was in Mexico, he saw his chance. He climbed into a car and drove across the **border** to the United States.

Before leaving, Livan asked Orlando to go with him. Orlando refused. He didn't want to leave his **homeland**.

When the team returned to Cuba without Livan, government officials blamed Orlando. They wanted to punish him for his brother's actions. They also wanted to make sure that he never defected. So they banned Orlando from baseball. He could no longer travel with the team, so he couldn't defect. Since Cuba is an island, he would have to cross the sea to get away. That wouldn't be easy. Besides, the police would be watching him closely.

The Need to Be Free

Orlando began to feel as if he was slowly dying. He couldn't play the game he loved. He had trouble sleeping. Worse, some people threw rocks at him. They believed he had turned against Cuba. "I feel great pain," said Orlando.

Livan Hernandez became a great pitching star in the United States.

Orlando Hernandez and his friends were rescued from the island.

Meanwhile, Orlando's half brother had become a great pitching star in the United States. Livan played for the Florida Marlins. In 1997 he led the team to a **World Series** win over the Cleveland Indians. He was was named the Most **Valuable** Player for the series.

At last, in 1997 Orlando and seven other people decided to escape. Their plans had to be kept secret. If the Cuban police found out, Orlando knew they would be put in jail for a long time.

The group planned to cross the Straits of Florida on a boat with a homemade sail. But the trip would be dangerous. Their boat was not strong. It leaked. It might fall apart in the middle of the sea. Orlando knew the group might drown or be eaten by sharks. But he and his friends never **hesitated**. Orlando said, "I was ready to row all the way here if necessary."

The eight friends took what they could. They had four oars in case the wind died down. They made a **compass** to help guide them. It didn't look very useful. It was made out of a bunch of old **magnets**. Still, it was the best they could do.

For food, they carried four cans of meat. They also took some old bread and brown sugar. They needed drinking water, too. So they filled a small container with water and brought it along.

El Duque, a pitcher for the Yankees, greets his fans.

A New Life

One night the eight friends climbed onto the boat. Soon after they set out to sea, a storm kicked up. Hour after hour they drifted on the rough sea. Big waves rocked their small boat. The up-and-down movement made them seasick. Several of them threw up.

Finally, after ten hours, they landed on a small island. It was one of many islands in the Bahamas. This small country is just a few miles off the southeast coast of Florida. The group had sailed 40 miles on the open sea.

No one lived on the island where they landed. So Orlando and his friends had to wait and hope that someone would rescue them. They had little food left. They became so hungry that some of them began eating seaweed. The group built a small hut out of palm branches. When a plane flew overhead, they all ran inside the hut. They feared that it might be the Cuban Air Force.

At last, after four days on the island, the United States Coast Guard found and rescued them. Orlando and his friends had made it. They were finally free.

Orlando soon became a pitcher for the New York Yankees. Like his brother, El Duque quickly became a favorite of American fans. In 1998 he even helped the Yankees win the World Series.

USE WHAT YOU KNOW

Read and Remember — Check the Events

Place a check in front of the three sentences that tell what happened in the story.

_____ **1.** Livan Hernandez helped his brother escape from Russia.

_____ **2.** El Duque was told that he would never again pitch in Cuba.

_____ **3.** Orlando Hernandez left Cuba in a leaky boat.

_____ **4.** Cuban leaders wanted El Duque to play basketball.

_____ **5.** El Duque and seven others landed on an island in the Bahamas.

_____ **6.** Orlando Hernandez was banned from the World Series.

Think About It — Find the Main Ideas

Underline the two most important ideas from the story.

1. Orlando Hernandez made $8.75 a month as a hospital worker.

2. Orlando Hernandez took many risks to reach freedom.

3. In 1995 Orlando Hernandez visited Mexico.

4. El Duque sailed across the open sea in an old boat.

5. Livan and Orlando Hernandez were half brothers.

6. In 1998 the Yankees won the World Series.

Focus on Vocabulary — Finish the Paragraphs

Use the words in dark print to complete the paragraphs. Reread the paragraphs to be sure they make sense.

banned	**homeland**	**hesitated**	**valuable**
border	**compass**	**World Series**	**salary**
magnets	**defect**		

The Hernandez half brothers were Cuban baseball players. In 1995 Livan Hernandez crossed the (1)_____ from Mexico to the United States. Cuban leaders were afraid Orlando Hernandez would try to (2)_____, too. So they (3)_____ him from playing baseball. They gave him a job with a (4)_____ of only $8.75 a month. Finally, Orlando decided that he had to leave his (5)_____. Once he made that decision, Orlando never (6)_____.

Orlando and seven friends climbed into a boat with a homemade sail. They needed a (7)_____ to help guide them. So they made one with some old (8)_____. The group survived a dangerous journey across the sea to the Bahamas. When Orlando finally got to the United States, he became a very (9)_____ pitcher for the Yankees. Orlando even helped his baseball team win the (10)_____.

Distance Scale

On a map, use a **distance scale** to find the distance between two places. The map below shows Orlando Hernandez's homeland, Cuba. The map's distance scale shows that 1 inch of the map stands for 125 miles of land and water. Use a ruler to measure the distances on the map. Circle the correct answer to each question.

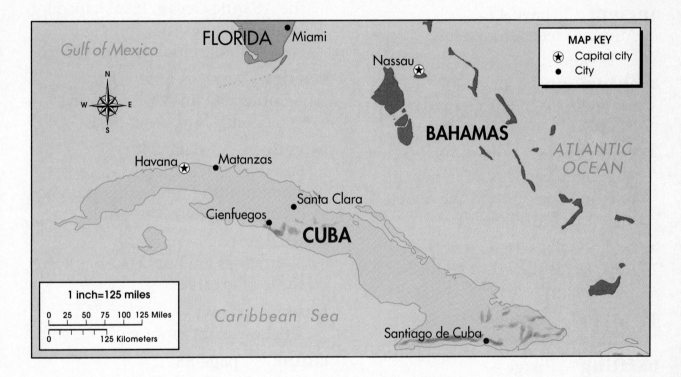

1. About how many inches are between Havana and Miami on the map?

   2 inches   4 inches   1 inch

2. What is the actual distance between Havana and Miami?

   250 miles   125 miles   325 miles

3. What is the actual distance between Matanzas and Santa Clara?

   250 miles   150 miles   110 miles

4. What city is about 350 miles from Havana?

   Cienfuegos   Santiago de Cuba   Nassau

GLOSSARY

🌐 Words with this symbol can be found in the USE A MAP activities.

active　page 82
Being active means being lively or moving around.

afloat　page 89
Afloat means floating.

ancient　page 47
Ancient means from a long time ago.

archipelago　page 50
An archipelago is a group of islands.

Arctic Circle　page 79
The Arctic Circle is an imaginary line that goes around the region near the North Pole.

arrest　page 16
An arrest is the act of taking someone prisoner.

attracted　page 89
Attracted means drew to oneself.

baffling　page 42
Baffling means confusing or hard to explain.

balsa　page 47
Balsa is a kind of wood that is very light but strong.

bamboo　page 48
Bamboo is a tall grass that looks like tubes made of thin wood.

banned　page 95
Banned means did not allow a person to do something.

belugas　page 79
Belugas are white whales that live in cold water.

Bermuda Triangle　page 39
The Bermuda Triangle is an area of the Atlantic Ocean. It is shaped by imaginary lines that run from Florida to Bermuda to Puerto Rico.

border　pages 53, 93, 96
🌐 A border is a line that separates two countries or other areas.

boredom　page 24
Boredom is what a person feels when nothing interesting is going on and life seems very dull.

boundaries　page 39
Boundaries are lines that mark the edges of an area.

bow　page 33
The bow is the front end of a ship.

canal　page 55
A canal is a kind of river made by people for use by boats.

cape　page 16
A cape is a point of land that sticks out into the sea.

capital city　page 72
A capital city is a city that serves as a center for the government of a state or a country.

capsized　page 57
Capsized means turned upside-down.

cargo   page 15
Cargo means goods carried by a ship, train, or airplane.

chain   page 90
A chain is a series of related objects, such as islands.

channel   page 32
A channel is a body of water that connects two larger bodies of water.

charted   page 7
Charted means made a map of a place.

churning   page 73
Churning means stirring up or shaking wildly.

civilization   page 47
A civilization is a place where people live and share customs.

classical   page 82
Classical music is music that has no words and follows certain rules.

clipper ship   page 15
A clipper ship is a ship that moves very fast and has large square sails.

collide   page 31
To collide means to bump or strike together.

compass   page 97
A compass is equipment used to show direction, such as north or south.

compass rose   page 21
🌐 A compass rose is a symbol on a map that shows direction.

concrete   page 87
Concrete is a mixture of cement, sand, and water. It is a strong building material.

continent   pages 7, 13
🌐 A continent is a very large body of land, such as Africa.

coral   page 7
Coral is the skeletons of many tiny sea animals packed together.

cove   page 25
A cove is a small area of water that is protected from wind by land.

crew   page 7
A crew is a group of people who work together on a ship.

currents   page 24
Currents are waters flowing in a certain direction.

defect   page 95
To defect means to run away from one's country.

degrees   pages 37, 69, 73
🌐 Degrees are units of measure for temperature or distance.

delayed   page 72
Delayed means put off until later.

depth   page 8
Depth is how deep something is.

desperate   page 88
Desperate means almost without hope.

distance scale   pages 61, 101
🌐 A distance scale compares distance on a map with distance in the real world.

elevations   page 85

🌐 Elevations are heights above a given level, such as sea level.

energy   page 90

Energy is the strength to do work.

equator   pages 16, 29

🌐 The equator is an imaginary circle that runs east and west around Earth. It divides Earth equally into north and south.

ferryboat   page 87

A ferryboat is a boat used to carry people, goods, and cars across short distances.

First Mate   page 16

The First Mate is the second most important officer on a ship. The captain is the top officer.

floes   page 79

Floes are huge chunks of ice floating in the ocean.

gulf   page 55

A gulf is a body of water that fills a large bend in the land.

Gulf Stream   page 71

The Gulf Stream is a warm water of the North Atlantic Ocean. It flows east past Florida.

harbor   page 48

A harbor is a place for ships to go where the water is deep and protected from bad weather.

harpoon   page 48

A harpoon is a long, sharp weapon connected to a rope. It is used to hunt fish.

headwaters   page 26

Headwaters are small streams that form the beginning of a river.

hemispheres   page 29

🌐 If the world is divided in half, it is divided into two hemispheres.

hesitated   page 97

Hesitated means waited or stopped because one is not sure.

homeland   page 96

A homeland is the area or the country where a person was born or grew up.

horrified   page 80

To be horrified is to be shocked, upset, or very afraid.

hurricane   page 57

A hurricane is a storm that has very strong winds and usually occurs with rain, thunder, and lightning.

iceberg   page 31

An iceberg is a huge block of floating ice.

icebreaker   page 81

An icebreaker is a ship that can cut a path through ice.

immediately   page 63

Immediately means right away.

immigrants   page 31

Immigrants are people who move to another country to live.

infection   page 71

An infection is a disease that is spread by a germ.

islanders	page 47
Islanders are people who live on islands.

jolt	page 88
A jolt is a sudden jerk or bump.

keys	page 72
Keys are small, low islands near shore.

latitude	pages 37, 69
🌐 Lines of latitude are imaginary lines that run east and west around Earth. They measure distance in degrees north and south of the equator.

lifeboats	page 31
Lifeboats are small boats used for saving lives.

lifeguard	page 87
A lifeguard is a person who works at a beach or a pool to save swimmers from drowning.

logbook	page 15
A logbook is a book in which the details of a ship's journey are written.

longitude	pages 37, 69
🌐 Lines of longitude are imaginary lines that run north and south around Earth. They measure distance in degrees east and west of the 0° longitude.

lookout	page 33
A lookout is a person who watches for signs of danger.

lurking	page 48
Lurking means moving or waiting in a sneaky way.

magnets	page 97
Magnets are pieces of metal or rock that attract iron or steel.

map key	page 45
🌐 A map key tells what the symbols, colors, or patterns on a map mean.

marathon	page 71
A marathon is a very long race.

mast	page 24
A mast is a tall pole that holds up a sail.

mine	page 41
A mine is a bomb hidden in the sea or in the ground.

mutiny	page 17
A mutiny is when a ship's crew refuses to obey the captain.

navigate	page 15
To navigate means to guide a ship.

officials	page 40
Officials are people in command.

Olympics	page 71
The Olympics are sports contests between different countries.

operation	page 81
An operation is an action planned out ahead of time.

outlaws	page 25
Outlaws are people who do not follow the law.

pack ice	page 79
Pack ice is large blocks of ice that are jammed together.

plunged	page 64
Plunged means pushed hard or with force into something.

port   page 17
A port is a place where ships go to load and unload goods.

pumps   page 10
Pumps are machines used to get water out of boats.

raft   page 47
A raft is a kind of flat boat that is sometimes made from wood.

reef   page 7
A reef is a line of rocks or coral just under or above the surface of the water.

regions   page 63
Regions are areas of land.

restless   page 26
Restless means not able to relax or stay still.

risking   page 23
Risking means putting oneself in danger of possible death or injury.

route map   page 77
A route map is a map that shows the roads and highways in an area.

salary   page 95
A salary is money that is paid for a person's work.

sandbar   page 23
A sandbar is an area of sand that builds up underwater.

scars   page 66
Scars are marks left on skin after cuts or other wounds have healed.

seasick   page 73
Seasick means feeling ill from being in or sailing on rough water.

shifting   page 81
Shifting means changing the place or direction of something.

shoreline   page 90
A shoreline is the line where land meets a body of water.

skipper   page 55
A skipper is a ship's captain.

S.O.S.   page 40
An S.O.S. is a call for help that is used by ships and airplanes.

spear   page 63
To spear is to pierce with a long, sharp weapon.

speargun   page 63
A speargun is a tool that shoots long, sharp weapons called spears.

stern   page 34
The stern is the back end of a ship.

stitches   page 66
Stitches are the threads that doctors sew into skin to close a wound.

strait   page 8
A strait is a narrow body of water.

submarines   page 41
Submarines are ships that travel underwater.

succeeded   page 58
Succeeded means completed as planned or desired.

surgeons   page 66
Surgeons are doctors who operate on people.

survived   page 34
Survived means stayed alive.

survivors page 58
Survivors are people who stay alive through a disaster, such as a storm or a flood.

terrifying page 56
Terrifying means very scary or alarming.

theory page 41
A theory is an idea used to explain how something happened.

tide page 9
A tide is the movement of the sea toward or away from land. A high tide is water rising high on the land.

torpedo page 41
A torpedo is an exploding weapon shot from a ship, submarine, or airplane.

unsinkable page 31
Unsinkable means not able to sink or go down.

valuable page 97
Valuable means very important.

vanish page 39
To vanish is to disappear suddenly.

vessel page 25
A vessel is a ship or large boat.

victim page 64
A victim is a person who is hurt or killed.

violent page 56
Violent means powerful.

voyage page 10
A voyage is a long trip by boat.

wet suit page 66
A wet suit is a rubber suit worn by a swimmer or diver to help keep him or her warm.

white squall page 56
A white squall is a rare storm that strikes without warning at sea.

World Series page 97
The World Series is a set of baseball games that are played to decide which American or Canadian team is the best that year.

Did You Know?

◀ Can you believe that 70 percent of Earth's surface is water, not land? Most of the water is in the four oceans. The Pacific Ocean is the largest of the four oceans. It covers more than 64 million square miles. There's enough water in just the Pacific Ocean to cover all seven continents!

Have you ever wondered how much salt is in seawater? Ocean water is about 3 percent salt. But the saltiest water on Earth is found in Israel's Dead Sea. The water in this saltwater lake is almost 10 times as salty as water in the oceans. In fact, the Dead Sea is so salty that people can float on the water without sinking! ▶

◀ Did you know that the largest animal in the world lives in the ocean? The largest animal is the blue whale. This animal is 10 times longer than an elephant!

Have you ever heard of a sea of seaweed? The Sargasso Sea is a giant sea of thick seaweed. This sea is found in the North Atlantic Ocean. The water in the Sargasso Sea is calm. That makes it easy for the floating plants to grow. The sea looks like a giant salad! ▶

◀ What is the biggest kind of wave? It is called the tsunami. This giant wave is caused by energy from an earthquake under the sea. A tsunami can be almost 100 feet high when it reaches shore. That's about as tall as a 10-story building. A tsunami can be so powerful that it can crush anything that is in its way!

Did you know that a swordfish can weigh as much as 1,500 pounds? That's as heavy as a small car! This big fish can actually move quite fast. It can swim up to 60 miles per hour in short bursts. That's as fast as a car traveling on a highway! ▶

CHART YOUR SCORES

Score Your Work

1. Count the number of correct answers you have for each activity.
2. Write these numbers in the boxes in the chart.
3. Give yourself a score (maximum of 5 points) for **Write About It**.
4. Add up the numbers to get a final score for each tale.
5. Write your final score in the score box.
6. Compare your final score with the maximum score given for each story.

Tales	Read and Remember	Think About It	Write About It	Focus on Vocabulary	Use a Map	Score
Into the Unknown						/26
Captain Mary						/26
Alone at Sea						/22
The Ship That Could Not Sink						/22
A Ship Lost						/26
101 Days at Sea						/24
Without Warning						/24
Shark Attack!						/26
A Dangerous Swim						/23
Whales in Trouble						/23
Lucky to Be Alive						/27
Escape to Freedom						/19

ANSWER KEY

Into the Unknown

Pages 6–13

Read and Remember — Finish the Sentence:
1. Australia 2. Great Barrier Reef 3. sinking
4. rising water 5. sail

Write About It: Answers will vary.

Focus on Vocabulary — Make a Word:
1. continent 2. charted 3. depth 4. pumps
5. voyage 6. coral 7. strait 8. reef 9. tide
10. crew. The letters in the circles spell *the Pacific.*

Use a Map — Continents and Oceans:
1. Pacific, Atlantic, Arctic, Indian oceans 2. Africa,
Australia, Asia, Europe, Antarctica, North America,
South America 3. Asia, Australia, Antarctica,
North America, South America 4. Indian Ocean,
Atlantic Ocean 5. Arctic Ocean 6. Atlantic Ocean

Captain Mary

Pages 14–21

Read and Remember — Choose the Answer:
1. South America 2. Joshua Patten 3. the First
Mate 4. cold and rough 5. help her 6. California

Think About It — Fact or Opinion:
1. F 2. O 3. O 4. F 5. F 6. O

Focus on Vocabulary — Finish the Paragraphs:
1. clipper ship 2. cargo 3. equator 4. cape
5. First Mate 6. arrest 7. port 8. mutiny
9. navigate 10. logbook

Use a Map — Map Directions:
1. south 2. Chile 3. northeast 4. southeast

Alone at Sea

Pages 22–29

Read and Remember — Check the Events:
Sentences 2, 3, 5

Write About It: Answers will vary.

Focus on Vocabulary — Finish Up:
1. vessel 2. outlaws 3. mast 4. currents
5. risking 6. headwaters 7. cove 8. sandbar
9. restless 10. boredom

Use a Map — Hemispheres:
1. Southern Hemisphere 2. Eastern Hemisphere
3. Northern and Western hemispheres 4. Western,
Southern, and Northern hemispheres

The Ship That Could Not Sink

Pages 30–37

Read and Remember — Finish the Sentence:
1. zero 2. New York 3. at night 4. women and
children 5. in lifeboats 6. North Atlantic Ocean

Think About It — Find the Main Ideas:
Sentences 2, 4

Focus on Vocabulary — Crossword Puzzle:
ACROSS — 1. collide 3. immigrants 4. unsinkable
7. lookout 8. stern 9. survived
DOWN — 1. channel 2. lifeboats 5. iceberg
6. bow

Use a Map — Latitude and Longitude:
1. 42°N 2. 0° 3. Cairo 4. Singapore

A Ship Lost

Pages 38–45

Read and Remember — Choose the Answer:
1. one engine 2. Bermuda Triangle 3. nothing
4. German attack 5. a mystery

Write About It: Answers will vary.

Focus on Vocabulary — Find the Meaning:
1. disappear 2. area of the Atlantic Ocean 3. lines
marking an area's edges 4. call for help 5. people
in command 6. hidden bomb 7. exploding rocket
8. underwater ships 9. idea 10. hard to explain

Use a Map — Map Keys:
1. ◉ 2. no 3. large city 4. Brunswick, Georgia,
and Myrtle Beach, South Carolina 5. Everglades
6. yes

101 Days at Sea

Pages 46–53

Read and Remember — Check the Events:
Sentences 3, 5, 6

Think About It — Drawing Conclusions:
Answers will vary. Here are some possible
conclusions.   1. The ancient Peruvians and the
islanders shared certain words, food, and beliefs.
2. He wanted to prove that the ancient Peruvians
could have made the journey.   3. A shark scared
him out of the water.   4. No one had ever seen the
rare fish alive before.   5. A large octopus could
attack and hurt them.

Focus on Vocabulary — Match Up:
1. f 2. a 3. i 4. c 5. g 6. b 7. e 8. j 9. h 10. d
Use a Map — Countries:
1. Lima 2. Trujillo, Arequipa, Iquitos 3. Ecuador
4. Brazil, Ecuador, Colombia, Bolivia, Chile
5. Andes Mountains 6. yes

Without Warning
Pages 54–61
Read and Remember — Finish the Sentence:
1. classroom 2. Gulf of Mexico 3. tip over
4. below deck 5. a lifeboat
Write About It: Answers will vary.
Focus on Vocabulary: Find the Meaning
1. river made by people 2. turned upside-down
3. deadly storm at sea 4. captain 5. strong, windy
rainstorm 6. completed as desired 7. people who
lived 8. very scary 9. water near a bend of land
10. powerful
Use a Map — Distance Scale:
1. $\frac{1}{2}$ inch 2. 100 miles 3. 250 miles 4. Managua

Shark Attack!
Pages 62–69
Read and Remember — Choose the Answer:
1. spearfishing 2. Australia 3. the eye 4. a rope
5. 462 stitches 6. diver
Think About It — Find the Sequence:
2, 1, 3, 6, 4, 5
Focus on Vocabulary — Make a Word:
1. plunged 2. surgeons 3. spear 4. scars 5. victim
6. wet suit 7. stitches 8. regions 9. immediately
10. speargun. The letters in the circles spell
Great White.
Use a Map — Latitude and Longitude:
1. Darwin 2. Perth 3. 35°S 4. Melbourne

A Dangerous Swim
Pages 70–77
Read and Remember — Check the Events:
Sentences 2, 3, 5
Write About It: Answers will vary.
Focus on Vocabulary — Match Up:
1. g 2. a 3. j 4. e 5. f 6. d 7. h 8. i 9. c 10. b

Use a Map — Route Map:
1. U.S. Highway 27 2. U.S. highway 3. Interstate
Highways 4 and 75 4. State Highway 70
5. U.S. Highway 41

Whales in Trouble
Pages 78–85
Read and Remember — Finish the Sentence:
1. fish 2. air holes 3. ice 4. the open sea 5. music
Think About It — Cause and Effect:
1. c 2. b 3. d 4. a
Focus on Vocabulary — Finish Up:
1. horrified 2. floes 3. icebreaker 4. belugas
5. pack ice 6. classical 7. active 8. shifting
9. Arctic Circle 10. operation
Use a Map — Elevation:
1. dark orange 2. 3,250–6,500 feet 3. Denali
4. Bethel

Lucky to Be Alive
Pages 86–93
Read and Remember — Choose the Answer:
1. It sank. 2. life jackets 3. her pants 4. sharks
5. a lollipop 6. by swimming
Write About It: Answers will vary.
Focus on Vocabulary — Crossword Puzzle:
ACROSS — 3. ferryboat 4. shoreline 5. attracted
8. concrete 9. lifeguard; DOWN — 1. desperate
2. jolt 5. afloat 6. chain 7. energy
Use a Map — Countries:
1. Jakarta 2. Vietnam 3. Thailand, Laos, Vietnam
4. South China Sea 5. yes 6. Indonesia

Escape to Freedom
Pages 94–101
Read and Remember — Check the Events:
Sentences 2, 3, 5
Think About It — Find the Main Ideas:
Sentences 2, 4
Focus on Vocabulary — Finish the Paragraphs:
1. border 2. defect 3. banned 4. salary
5. homeland 6. hesitated 7. compass 8. magnets
9. valuable 10. World Series
Use a Map — Distance Scale:
1. 2 inches 2. 250 miles 3. 110 miles 4. Nassau